How To Keep A Black Man

Jarray Walker

How to Keep a Black Man

Copyright © 2020 by Jarray Walker

To contact the author, email jarraywalker@yahoo.com.

Unless otherwise noted, all Scripture quotations are taken from www.blueletterbible.org.

Word definition taken from www.lexico.com or www.werriam-webster.com unless otherwise noted as the author's defined definition — (SD).

Cover design by: Denise Barringer

ISBN:

Printed in the United States of America.

Dedication

I would like to dedicate this book to ALL who seek answers on "How to Keep a Black Man." It doesn't matter the race nor gender. You will know by the end of this book the "Hows" and "Whys," and it will help you be successful on your journey. I dedicate this book to everybody who needs clear understanding of a man. This is for growth and longevity. This book is also for men who need to understand themselves. This is for open minded women and men; people who are willing to learn or better themselves.

NO MATTER WHAT RACE... NO MATTER WHAT SEX...THIS IS DEDICATED TO YOU ALL!

Acknowledgement

I want to acknowledge my team. All those who fall under the team, which is team D.E.BS, y'all know who you are. I want to thank y'all so much for all of the hard work that you put in to make this happen; all of the long nights of typing and days of brainstorming. We created a masterpiece and the world will know exactly who y'all are soon. I would also like to take the time to acknowledge my lovely aunt Aduke who helped me come up with the idea while walking through the streets of Hollywood. We did it! I stuck to the plan.

Table of Contents

How to Keep a Black Man

I realize that I will get many "homie WTF" looks about this book. So, I hope y'all do something with it, let it help you overcome and learn from your past problems. This book is written from the point of view of two black men for women, and it'll help any sex looking to be with that right man. There is no discrimination. It is what it is in my eyes.

We have to understand that we have all types of people around us; straight, gay, bisexual, heterosexual, transgender, curious, or experimenting. Whatever you represent is what you represent. No one can judge. If this book can help you understand your partner, that's great. If this book can help only one person to understand their partner, then my mission has been accomplished.

Chapter One

Professional Black Man

How are you, ladies? I am the professional black man. I get up early every morning, shower, watch the news, read the newspaper, and eat. I expect to smell breakfast being cooked and prepared. I also look for my suit and tie to be ironed and ready so I can be sharp and as professional as possible. I tell the woman I'm with that I love her if that is where we are in a relationship. Then, I kiss her before going to work. My goal is to have a better day than yesterday.

I focus on leaving the bad in the past and the good in the future. If we were mad at each other last night, I don't want to hear it again the next day. Leave the bad feelings behind. Don't be stank the following day. All it will do is make our day sour because you want to dwell on petty things from 24 hours ago. Remember everything you do after a disagreement, to be petty, does nothing but turn me off. My goals are to work and try to make sure we can live a better life.

I love that you work or go to school, that is a must. You have to do one or the other or both. I love for you to be my equal. I don't care if you make more or less, as long as you have independent traits. You must keep yourself up. Of course, I will help because I love it when you wear certain hairstyles and clothes. I will make sure that if I'm on top of my game, my woman most definitely is. My goal is to secure our future and make sure we have any and every source we need to succeed.

I live to be an honest man and forever be a strong, hardworking protector. I'm a strong man that will go over bars set for me and mine! I will do everything in my power to make sure we are good. I strive to be very intelligent. I transform knowledge into wisdom. I will never be content when it comes to bettering myself and anyone that I'm with. I am the handy that will do what's manly around the house. However, I will also teach my lady and kids how to do the same in case something happens to me. When I'm done giving you the tools, you will not have to depend on another man for too much of nothing. Fortunately, I'm not leaving Earth any time soon. So, I'll still be doing those things.

Chapter Two

Invest

It's hard to invest in a relationship when one never knows if it will even make it until the next day. I don't mind taking a woman out or spoiling her. I might even get her a gift here and there. But anything huge, I think there should be an establishment; strength in the relationship. I feel like I can't invest in something, especially financially, if there's a constant sign of separation. The separation can be mental or physical. Say I pay off your house or car and tomorrow you decide we're not going to be together. Now that leaves a man like me looking stupid and used. I need to feel security just as much as a woman that wants to be protected.

We cannot fault one another on our past or our insecurities. We can not bring someone new into our lives with the perception of the fault of another before them when they walk through the door. It's very unfair and can run your blessings away just as fast as winning your eye. The way I look at things is I don't care about your past mistakes, and you are holding on to some of them. I do realize there are things of importance as far as your overcoming and moving on. This doesn't mean that I don't care about certain things because your past holds some importance. But understand, I do not judge your past. Only God can. I don't fault you for it. Instead, I do it very differently. I start your new past the day I meet you. So, if I meet you at 1:30 p.m. and it's now 1:35 p.m., you're 5 minutes into your past.

We, as humans, are not perfect. Adam and Eve proved that we do stuff in our lives that qualify as mistakes. We all have done things we can say we are not proud of. Some have regrets. Some of us know how horrible of a word that is to us. So, you might as well get it in your head that no one has a perfect non-regretful mistake-free life. Why judge stuff we had no experience in? What about the things that you've done that can be judged and be prosecuted for? We can't put people through double jeopardy. We have to ask ourselves how we would feel if God judges us on our past out of disgust. We would want Him to forgive us and not hold it against us, right? I know it seems that I jumped in without sugar coating. If it comes out while I'm writing, so be it.

Everything links together. When we are together in a relationship, we have to show and make our presence known. Like I say, we can't fault someone who doesn't want to invest in uncertainty. If we agree as friends, it's much easier. There's more understanding, and the investment isn't so crazy. Shit, my friend and I fought each other, have been mad at each other, but we know we will always be cool. That's what friends do. Always keep it real with no B.S. If you can't be with someone, just be friends until it works out.

On another note, let me give a few examples of investment separation. I may fall back on other women when I'm dealing with someone. Yes, I am a freak when it comes to my woman or that exclusive person that I'm dealing with. So, I say things to her like, "Baby, you're a queen. That thing is supposed to be eaten every day, even on some lunch breaks." She loves the idea because she's supposedly a freak right along with me. She's always screaming, "Babe, if you want some oral or sex, just let me know. Don't go without it". She says this because sometimes I just want her to go home and relax from a hard day of work, but she says she would rather make sure I'm good or whatever. So, time goes on, and I still let her go home from work if we're not living together.

Later, I say our code. "Like damn, babe, I should've caught you before you went home. I want some loving." (Our code for oral.) She texts back, "Was that appropriate? What am I a slut to you or something?" I reply, "Huh?" Then she says, "Really? You should've got your dick sucked before I went home. Are you serious?" No response needed.

So, I didn't say it the way she took it. She was just in her feelings about something, and now all of a sudden, I'm disrespecting her. I can't deal with wishy-washy women. I said it very appropriately, and when I finally asked, she blew up. Yet she's the same one who wanted to have sex outside knowing people can see. The reaction that she gave me turned me off completely. I was no longer interested in being with her in a sexual way at that moment. I felt like she was overreacting. She had a bad day or something which she could have communicated. That wasn't the case, though. For some reason, she was seriously angry because I asked for oral sex. Now, she has me like the second dude in this book. Feeling like she can just kick rocks and go about her way and just do her, which leads me to tell you more of the things that make us not want to be with you.

There was another thing that occurred that was so petty and very childish to me. This happened after we had a conversation about respecting each other as we were trying to build something together. She tells me a man was hired at her job, but there is nothing to worry about. She's focused. Plus, it had previously come up about females jocking me as a professional man, which is understandable. She knows I'm good with not entertaining other women. Nothing they do really strikes my interests or makes me want to indulge. I noticed that she went on to tell me that he wears Tims, jeans, T-shirts and looks masculine.

TIMEOUT! She truly messed up there! That showed me her eyes

are taking in descriptive detail. I kept my cool. I reminded her that by being his boss he has to follow her around. "Yes," she said. "Don't think anything of it if you see a black guy wearing Tims and a wife beater following me around the store." TIMEOUT! HA! HA!

I try to explain that eventually he's going to try her especially with her being his boss. He's going to say to himself, "Damn, if I get her on my team, I'm good." I reminded her that's what many men may try because she's beautiful. We went from her starting this whole conversation about respect to her, asking, "What? Am I a hoe or something?" Now, I'm thinking that she's tripping.

I ask, "How do you get mad because I'm just telling you how men are and what he may try?" She kept going, so eventually, I snapped. I couldn't figure out how did she get defensive about me talking about him? You're guilty about something it seems. Ladies, do not be petty. It ruins relationships and it's very damaging to your resume. These are a few reasons and examples as to why you can't keep a black man. Things like these are reasons men cheat, do what they do and don't care. I don't care how you ask me for sex, you're getting it. Plus I'm not letting the next man get it.

There is no need to be petty because if you were explaining to your man how women were, it would be you giving him signs to watch out for. Therefore, you're helping him to get ahead of the game and keep what is being secured from outside dangers and temptations. I feel if your significant other feels some type of way about your loyalty you should make them feel comfortable about the situation. Assure them that everything is fine and that there's no other man. Applying the negative things I mentioned before are great ways to push a good, strong black man such as myself further away.

Chapter Three

Change It Up

Sex is so important because I have to be physically attracted to a woman to be with them the right way. What do I mean by the right way? A man can love a woman, be in love with her, and look to her as his forever. However, he cannot be physically into her or lose his drive in this department. If he isn't all there physically, then that can lead to him going elsewhere sexually. That doesn't mean he's into the new woman because she has nothing in all the other departments, but physically there's a connection. I will get into the other departments later on. My writing will come together like a puzzle.

By him having to go elsewhere, he's not with you the way he is supposed to be. The good news is if he was once into you heavy in that area, you can fix it or keep it that way. How? Change up your approach to the things you usually do. Get sex toys and try some stuff. Get him off the couch if you can and take him somewhere so that you both can look at things that both of you will enjoy. Pay attention to what puts glitter in his eyes. If it doesn't, keep trying until you see it because you will.

Catering also helps in that area. Have him a candlelit bath when he comes home or his favorite food cooked. If you can't cook, then learn. Rub his feet, back, neck, and shoulders. Shit, grab his private part, and stroke it some. As a matter of fact, do a full body massage when he gets out of the bathtub. Have the baby oil ready and lay him down on top of some towels on the bed. Then rub him down. Massage him like you're more into it than he is. Trust, he'll feel the sincerity. Shit! He'll probably be rock hard without you touching him. If not, no worries. I bet he's going to get to that point. You're telling him without saying it that you love him and that he's King.

When he gets out of the bathtub, make sure the bedroom candle is lit or smelling good as hell. Make him lay on his stomach. Tell him, "It's massage and moisturizing time." You should be in a robe. Take it off and give it to him naked. As you rub him, lean in and kiss him on the neck with your twins brushing against him real seductively! Give him a good bit of time in each area. Don't rush as you work your way down. I don't know if he'll let you massage his off-limits. Make your judgment, but massage his nuts from down there. He may jump, but he'll definitely let out a few moans.

Continue to rub and stroke him and then turn him over. Do the same, but stay on him, kiss him, but keep massaging while working your way down. If you're feeling freaky, sneak in some oral. When it's ready, you'll know. All nice and hard. Hop on it. Take a ride around the corner and back, but do not let him do anything! He's going to want to take over, but don't let him. Continue to do you. Then feed him. He'll go to sleep thinking and plotting on how he's going to get you back. There are many ways to keep it interesting with the change-up.

The Truth about the Vagina

Everything that I discuss in this section is my perception, opinions, and from my personal experiences. Most women think that the P is so powerful, and it's just automatic. Women are always screaming how they want a big ole dick. They say can't no little dick please them or do anything for them. They also speak about how they can feel nothing because it's too small or whatever. The reason it's not enough for you is because you don't know how to use your vagina properly. What do I mean? Just like a man's dick, the vagina is a muscle that needs to be exercised to be able to control the movement fully.

Why is this important? It's simple. If you learn how to control the vagina, it should be able to fit any size dick. I bet if you go to start giving oral sex, your lips can fit his penis, right? Why though? Because you can control your mouth and squeeze like an anaconda if you want to make it tight-fitting for his penis. Well, the vagina is a pair of lips with the ability to do the same thing, contract those muscles. It can stretch for a big penis, and it can contract for a small one. If you can't do this then maybe, it's been pushed past its limits.

You have to get its muscles back working in order. To do that, you can do an exercise called Kegel. Kegel is an exercise to strengthen the pelvic floor muscles in which the levator muscles are squeezed and held for five seconds and then released for five-seconds for several reps. (1) They are used to treat urinary incontinence or to prepare for a recovery from childbirth. When you get this down to a science, any penis should be able to do. Well, most should be able to make you feel some type of way. Maybe some are way too small, and it's just beyond normal. Then perhaps there is nothing you can do to make it work for both of you—another thing. You can't complain that a man is too small because it's really the vagina that is the problem.

If you think about it, women squeeze out whole babies a billion times the size of a penis. Some even squeeze out more than one at a time. Some squeezed out a few over the course of a few years. So, of course, no man can truly hurt the vagina. You can hit things that shouldn't be hit, but not hurt the vagina. So, ladies stop the madness. Most women and men don't really know or realize that the vagina actually has three different sexual points. Those points are called the A-spot, U-spot, and G-spot. The A-spot is beyond the G-spot just above the cervix and can be located during anal sex. It's known as the equivalent of the male prostate. However, it can be found during PIV penetration and foreplay as well. In my opinion, only eleven percent of women have discovered this zone.

How do you stimulate the spot? Make sure your nails are trimmed and cleaned. Be sure to lubricate your fingers and insert them into the deepest point of the vagina. Once you locate a round and firm area in the vagina, you have reached the cervix. You will then move your finger gently over that area. Since the A-spot is located in the back of the vagina, your finger or anal sex can hit that spot. Know that it doesn't always mean a long dick can hit that spot because the vaginas average length is below three inches. Therefore, it's possible to hit it with different positions and penetration.

The key to the orgasm is pressure, not necessarily movement. The U-spot is above the vagina, opening above the lips that can be stimulated with fingers and tongues. This spot has been discovered just from him rubbing his penis up and down the labia. The U-spot can be aroused with fingers and gentle movement across it, not pushing on it. Oral sex is one of the best ways to trigger the U-spot. Because it's already wet, it has less friction. However, the easiest way to find it is to open up the vagina with your tongue and licking upwards towards the clit. The G-spot is located an inch from the vagina opening on the upper vagina wall closer to the belly button.

The G-spot is sensitive, enduring stimulation swells. In my experience, some women have orgasms, and only a small percentage ejaculate when their G-spot is stimulated. To reach the G-spot, place your finger in a curl, and then in your vagina at least three inches deep inside, then you should be able to feel your G-spot. Some believe sex should not or isn't supposed to go past six to eight minutes because it damages the vagina, causing it to possibly lose its wetness. So, don't be running around here with a damaged vagina thinking you're supposed to have sex for hours. Instead of holding back when you feel your orgasm or ejaculation point because of your greed of wanting more, just let go!

Menstruation is a woman's monthly bleeding cycle. A regular natural change that occurs in a woman's reproductive system. Every woman's cycle isn't the same. Years after menstruation starts, some women's cycles could be long, but that is common. Why is this so important? During this time, you need to be very creative, especially when you're involved. The temptation of sex is very high during this time, and you do not want to leave him waiting and miserable. So, yes, you may have to give a lot of oral sex. You can even prep yourself depending on him also to explore other spots, spots that can satisfy both of you while your cycle is on.

Remember the U-spot? Yes, you guessed it. Don't squeeze up your face until you have at least tried the act thoroughly. You have to be a freak because trust me when you're not other women are. It triggers the interest of a man's curiosity, especially if you're in the I don't want to be bothered or touched stage, even when you don't want oral sex. What if your oral stage isn't all that he wants it to be? Try anal if you're about that life. Maybe he is, or perhaps he isn't. But it's another tool to hold him down until the monthly cycle has ceased.

Some guys, believe it or not, aren't into oral sex. Which is weird to me, but it's the truth. So, what if oral sex is the thing you relied on to get him through, but that isn't what he likes. Then what? I believe a very low percentage of black women have tried or even enjoyed anal sex back in the day. I think that during the modern times a high percentage of women participate in it and actually like it. I think many have also caught themselves wanting to do it.

In my opinion, women do not realize that they can have an orgasm from anal penetration through your vagina without vagina penetration. The trick to it is communication and having that person who is gentle and patient with the ins and out— LITERALLY! It is not a must that you do it or try it, but if you have great chemistry, I would recommend it. You might love it. A lot of women that I've talked to say they've had their best orgasms through anal penetration. Do not knock it until you've tried it successfully.

Take your time and work yourself into penetration. You may need to try fingers or plugs first and make sure he's taking your mind off it. He can do things like maybe sucking your breasts or fingering your vagina. That way, it'll loosen you up and not have you so tense. Don't be afraid to change it up!

Chapter Four

Levels of Friendship

Gaining a friendship is very important. There's level to relationships. In the growth and strength of it, for me as a GROWN ASS man, I have to see certain characteristics of a woman or let's say from a woman. Some stages have to be completed to have a successful lockdown relationship truly. Only one big one for me can be a deal-breaker and that is a lack of friendship; it is number one. It has to work.

We have to be able to work. We have to be that before anything extra can be attempted. If we can't be friends, how can we be together? To me, it's impossible because even in a relationship you have to still be a friend. A friend is someone who you can trust or are supposed to be able to trust. You should be able to talk to them about things without them getting into their feelings; such as getting mad about his feelings towards the things he may be going through. It'll help the both of you find each other's uniqueness.

Both of you have to want to be a friend to each other. It's not just one-sided. If I can't talk to you without you getting all in your feelings, getting mad, you not wanting to speak or so on. How can we communicate? That means I got to keep a lot from you which can lead to someone else being able to slide in and be a good listener. Now, there's a bond formed between the two. Of course, I am referring to a woman, but it could be someone at work, church, or in the neighborhood. Do not allow that to even occur.

It is possible to have a strong friendship. Be a good listener, give opinions and advice, but be true as a friend. Sometimes in life, well, it should be all the time. You got to be real about things and not say things you don't believe or give advice you would never accept and apply. It's nothing like being able to talk to a woman about things. Mainly because women are considered to be good listeners. How do you think you all are able to recite a whole conversation almost a year later? This too will be addressed in the next chapter.

Women's biggest problem is that they hear the word friend in a relationship with a man with negative perception. They believe that friends are equivalent to disrespect or downing them. It's really not a positive in most situations because 90 percent of women want more. They want a different title than friends. It's like the words "fuck friends" sounds better. I think during the last past 10-15 years people have made a complete mess of the word friends. It's no such thing nowadays. Even with regular friendships that consist of both sexes. It's like the new term is associates and that is not the same. Associates handle each other with long-handled spoons. So that means there's a limit to what is between the two.

Friend: a person who one knows and with whom one has a bond of personal or mutual affection. (2)

Associate: Allow oneself to be connected with or seen to be supportive of. (3)

Which do you fall under? Which would you rather fall under? We tend to use words and make them seem like it represents something, but we do not use them correctly all the time. So, if I say, "Oh, she's my associate. Somebody I deal with" that's less than being a friend. In fact, it's saying they are a non-attractive person I would never claim, especially in public. If I can't say you're my friend, that means you're worth nothing to me whatsoever in my eyes. If I say let's start as friends, that is a plus.

It's a compliment and it's huge to be considered to be someone's friend. To me, friends also mean do or die. I'm with you and got your back during any and everything. It means I trust in you with personal info and things in my life, things that can probably ruin my life. Nevertheless, I believe and have faith that you will stand strong and will always be in my favor as well as best interest. I do not expect you to be a yes person, though. I need someone to let me know when I am slipping or when I am making good or bad decisions.

For me, it's level to "Ships." We have to succeed in a friendship before anything. Which I've already explained what goes with that title. It's imperative to take these steps to let me know what my next step is. Now, if that becomes and turns out to be successful, it goes to the next level.

Relationships

Relationships for me means trying to make it an "us". It's more exclusive than friends. It's a bond. There are more obligations than a friend and creates more rights to each other. Only two can be active in this "ship." That is better known as "relationship". A lot of your freedom is taken away but can be for the good. If it's obvious, you've passed the start of the ships. It's a verbal understanding but amongst each other vow. It's not quite godly, but borderline. Which will be explained later.

Now, I'm not saying every professional good man has an exact mind state as me, but these tools are almost guaranteed to work. It all depends on the type of man that you tend to draw the attention of. When you get into a relationship with me, then that means we both have things to bring to the table. We have to be mirrored to each other on how we handle and respect the relationship. Nothing should be done that you don't want to be done to you. Wasting time is not permitted. No one has time for temporary situations. You have to make everything count. Do as you would like done to you. Of course, everything stated should go both ways, which leads to communication.

Communication

The definition of communication is "a process by which information is exchanged between individuals through a common system of symbols, signs, or behavior." (4) It is a means of connection between people or places in particular. Many problems can be solved with communication. Communication can have both a negative or positive effect on our lives. It is the biggest key to a successful relationship. However, it has to be used correctly. Sometimes the best way to communicate is silence and listening. I believe it's the key to anything you want to accomplish in life. It is an art you have to master it for it to work. It isn't as easy as it seems.

Just because you can talk or spell doesn't mean you automatically know the art of great communication. You can literally almost win any situation that you are placed in with excellent communication. If you feel like you can't talk to someone and it seems like the conversation always goes left or never works out, it could be that your communication is off or maybe it's because you need to come up with a completely different approach. Communication is essential, so it will be brought up many times in this book as you go forward.

Chapter Five

A Woman of Independence

Nothing makes me happier than a woman that goes to get her own. She doesn't depend on anyone. She is not going to sit around and have to figure out how to pay her bills or go through her phone, if it's still activated, to see who she can find to pay her bills because she feels she doesn't have to get a job. Now, I know most women dream of not having to work and not worry about bills. She just wants to be able to go shopping, get her hair, nails, and feet done. And if she has to cook, it's only every now and then.

She wants to drive around in her Mercedes and be pretty with an account that has plenty of money in it. While the man works hard to take care of everything because "that's what men are supposed to do," or so they say. A woman feels they shouldn't have to worry about anything at all. I agree, but that is different from not contributing to the price of living. Independence is essential. It's important because of the way life is today. It's not how it used to be 20 to 40 years ago. If the woman is a woman that depends and feels she shouldn't have to work, what's going to happen if the boyfriend/husband goes to jail? What if he gets killed? What if he loses his job or gets hurt where he can't work for an extended period of time?

There are a few outcomes to answer these questions. She can be a grown-ass, independent-minded woman, get a job and hold it down until the man gets back going or until times are better. She could show that she's with him through the good and bad. Show that she has his back and is willing to put in the work and be a go-getter, ensuring that everything will be ok. Or she could already have a job and be already putting forth what's needed to be sure that they'll never fall and live comfortably.

Another answer to those questions can be completely different. Say her man did go to jail and get time or whatever. If she's not independent, I can very well say that he has lost her maybe by sentencing and hopefully not before. She'll have a replacement before he gets shipped off to wherever he's going? Why? Because someone has to get these bills paid, keep her on fleek, and someone has to handle all of her needs. Guess what? You can no longer do it because you're not in the picture. Ladies, I can't entirely blame you for the way that you are because you have been spoiled. I still place blame on the fellas also. Yes, fellas. I have to be the realest. I can't withhold it because I'm a man. I have to show you, ladies, how to keep a black man, a GOOD ONE at that!

I place partial blame on the fellas because you have a lot of dudes that spoil females as such. I've seen men not want the woman to work but to be a stay at home girlfriend, wife, or whatever the case may be. I've also seen men try to make up the time lost with her by getting them gifts and giving them money, which can lead to them becoming spoiled. Yes, men sometimes do it to blind their women from things that they are doing or not doing. It is bad footing on who and how you want her to become or be. Show her how to get money. If she wasn't taught, put her on game so that she can know how to work or get money if need be.

I want a woman that comes with her own to the table like a job, career goals, bank account with cash saved up of her own. Not to sound thuggish, but I want a woman that only wants a man for dick, meaning she has everything else. She needs nothing. I believe the woman should take care of the small bills. The small statements are necessities such as phone bills, car insurance, food, and toiletries, little things as such. There's no problem with the man paying the rent and light and making sure the cars are working properly. The point is, ladies, make sure you practice and build your stage of independence.

While I'm talking about it, some of the things that I like is when the woman has her own money and says, "Let me take you out." Or when she offers to leave a tip when the man pays the bill. It's not that we're looking for it. It's just the thought that counts. Say he takes you out on a date. Y'all go to dinner, watch a movie, and may have dessert. If you leave a five-dollar tip, that's nothing to what he has paid. Even if he says, "No, you're good" and insists that everything is ok. Show him that five dollars are nothing. It's bigger than a tip. It shows that you have his back. Don't get stuck in those back in the day ways or those TV fairytale ways of feeling like you aren't supposed to do anything. It's more to it. You have to be an equal match. Match what he brings. When I say match, I don't mean the amount. I mean to be that mirror, as said before, which leads me to CAREERS!

Careers

Ladies, this is important because everyone growing up has a dream. Everyone wants to be something or like someone. Everyone has something they want to do for a living. No one should stray away from that. You still want to grow in time and accomplish what you've always set yourself out to do. This is said because no one should be out here with no direction and trying to figure how to pay bills or who will pay them. Then there will be no way that you are not independent or at least independent-minded. The reason for schooling is to help get through life or find great jobs.

Women already have a disadvantage just as much as we do with certain things in life. It said that we, as black men, would be dead or in jail. It is also said that men are better at everything than women and that women cannot succeed with certain things and jobs. So, the main goal should be beating the odds, not being a part of it.

For women, it said that they are gold diggers and that they just use men. Again, why not make that an opinion and not a proven fact. Do not be a part of that class. To me, it's a proven fact that a woman thinks better than a man with a certain percentage because a lot of men are on different levels of thinking. I hate to say it, but some can't even think. I believe it is a proven fact that a woman is a lot more level headed. This can follow under thinking, but it's slightly different. Men might think, but when it comes to things such as drama or altercation, he may not make the best decisions. So why not go to school, excel, get in a career, get your own money, and everything you need so that you can be equal.

When you're dependent on a man, you lose value as a woman. You're more like a child again. You're waiting on him to feed you, buy you clothes and shoes, waiting to get your hair done, and even waiting on your weekly allowance, not being able to do things when you want

—only being able to do something when he's ready for you to do it. What will you do for the holidays? Use the money that he gave you to get him a gift? Now he's looking crazy when he sees what you've got him. Only to realize that he has provided you with more money that brought him a gift. It's like he should've gone to the store himself. Well, actually, he did. You just saved him a trip. Not to mention, now he has to put gas in your car because you're low on fuel.

Does it feel good to always ask for money when you need something? Soon he will begin to say, "No, I don't have it because you're spending too much money." The crazy thing about it is that I know women are going to say this money's ours. But what you don't understand is that bills have to be paid. So now all of the things you want and need is probably not going to happen because there is no extra money. He is basically working like a slave to get things taken care of.

Why not help? Why not work? Some women will say if he does not have a good job, I cannot be with him. When the truth is, he does not need to be with you because you are in it for the wrong reasons. At least he has a job. Some men don't have two pennies to their name at all. You will be the type to help spend the money when it comes in. In fact, you may get a man that has some cash, and y'all are living it up. As soon as the money is gone, you're the type to vanish right along with it.

Now you've successfully turned a good, hardworking man into a broke and sad man because he knows that you are good and he's broke. When in all actuality, you could have helped build the future and have a good professional man that is happy and can continue with his success. Instead, you would rather live as an anchor to someone's life. I guess all ships have anchors. Don't come into a man's life and destroy what he is working so hard to build. I need someone that can grab a shovel and help me build an empire.

As I said earlier, don't be a child in my life. Be my equal. That way, you can stand on the side of me and not behind me. Don't be one of those that feel she can run the show with my money or my payday. Be the one that comes up with ways to run it up and accumulate more. Be that woman and prove to the world that women can hold it down to. That woman can be successful also. That woman can provide too. Show your worth. If all you have are two sets of lips, that is not going to work for my background check. Those are not just the tools that qualify to be anywhere near me. I can get that for $20, and that's all it will cost me. Your two sets of lips will probably cost me my whole body of success and some. That is not worth it, but a woman with worth is. In fact, it would be more genuine knowing she's good and has her own at the ending of the day.

Being a dependent girlfriend is not a career. It's a bill which I should be able to claim you on taxes. You should be a tax write-off. Just be great! Be a go-getter, but do it the right way. Let no one or a T.V. program have you thinking you should be or do anything different. I'm just saying that I am not looking to be a father to you or an ATM. So…be a woman of independence!

Chapter Six

Attitudes & Nagging

Where do I start? I do not like it. To me, it's like a big kid that cannot have their way. I think this is something that can be a deal-breaker for me after a while. I don't know what it is or why most woman chose to do it. But...we hate it. From experience, I've seen women wake up out of their sleep with an attitude. Sometimes it makes no sense at all as to why. For example, we go out and had dinner, watched a movie, and finished it off with long crazy wild sex. Shit, I even snatched her soul from her and also put her asleep. I nodded off after.

So, tell me, how is it you wake up in your feelings after a night like that? Like, what took place between you sleeping and waking up? At that moment I don't understand. So, I asked you if you were good, but all I got was a short eye-rolling answer, "Yup." What am I missing? Now I begin to think to myself, "I don't have time for this bipolar type shit." Yes, I can see if something happened the night or day before, and you happened to go to sleep mad about whatever it was. That would be understandable if that were the case. It's like women, well, let's say some suffer from bipolar ways or multiple personality issues.

So now, after we part ways for the day whether we're going to work or to our individual homes, that's when the text message starts rolling in—not a regular text, but a text the size of a book. That's what it feels like I'm about to read. It's like she had constructed it already and just pasted it from her phone because there is no way that she is typing that fast. It was like she already had it saved for a time like this. Sometimes I think to myself, "Is it this dick that got her in her feelings?"

Now let's break down a few scenarios that could cause this bipolar behavior. Maybe it could be that she and the guy are just friends, and she wants more from him as in a commitment. Perhaps it's because she feels all he likes about her is her sex and nothing else. But, if they are in a relationship or married, what else could it be. Maybe she is not fully satisfied? Perhaps her heart is not really with you or with someone else?

Could it be that it was so good that she started thinking about the past things that she said nothing about and they've resurfaced? I've seen women get mad at themselves because of things like the man not getting off during sex. So now, she feels like something is wrong with her. Maybe she feels like he's not attached as much as he used to be. Perhaps it's because she looks at you go work out every day and feels she's hot on every level but not all the way there body wise. Or maybe she woke up and saw him naked and asked herself, "Why won't he train me?" or invite me to the gym. Or perhaps she could just be crazy as hell and doesn't know why she is in her feelings. I don't know, ladies. Sometimes it just feels that you all stay with an attitude. It is just like we can never get things right. These things could leave a man confused as hell, not knowing what's going on.

Nagging: constantly harassing someone to do something. (5)

Nag: Annoy or irritate (a person) with persistent fault-finding or continuous urging. (6)

Just like an attitude, this is another thing that I could not deal with for an extended period of time. Something that will definitely drive a man crazy as hell is nagging. Especially since a woman can completely run out with it. Some of the worst times you could choose to nag a man to death that would probably cause a problem would be as soon as a man gets home from working 10-15 hours. Sometimes we just want to sit back and have a beer, a pack of cigarettes, or whatever else we need to calm us down. Instead, we come home to you nagging about what took us so long and why we just now came back. Saying things like, "Where have you been? You didn't come straight home from work" or complaining about things that happened yesterday that could've been discussed yesterday. Now you have your hands pointing in his face telling him what he needs to do or what is going to happen at a time where he just really needs peace of mind.

There are many wrong times to nag a man; when he finally decides to step out with his boys, enjoying watching the game in his man cave, at work, working mad as hell, and is ready to go upside somebody's head. It's even worse when you decide to start calling him a hundred times nagging about a lot of stupid things that can wait until later when he's off. It's annoying when you are calling while I'm shooting pool, asking me a bunch of nothing just to hear my background. Asking crazy questions like is there any woman there and insisting that I need to come home. I am always at home. I'm always under her. What she forgets to remember is that I'm a man also. So yes, I want to kick it with the fellas. So, when I do, don't nag me by blowing up my phone about nothing! Especially when you know that I'm coming home.

I mean, ladies, let us know. Is it that you can't help it? Is it something that you do on purpose? Like, do you sit there and say, "Today I'm going to get on his nerves?" Why continuously do things like nagging? That is going to piss us off. Having random attitudes and nagging can damage your relationship. A lot of men will try dealing with it at first. A lot of men will start to go off on you because they're tired of it. A lot of men will just leave for a while to blow steam. It may take a few hours, a day or two, or even worse, he may just call it quits. You have to be careful with these things because it can put you in a hole that you can't get out of.

Even if he doesn't leave, his whole attitude will change towards you. It will go from loving you and wanting to be around you to just putting up with you. Trust me that is something you do not want. That alone will only open windows of opportunity for outsiders to come in and be what you use to be when y'all first met. They'll be his air. They'll be his peace of mind. Now he does not want to be home because he knows all he is going to get is attitude and nagging, which leads to a million problems.

Don't nag or bother me because I'm working hard all the time or just plain always working. Especially if you're just a stay at home girl, he agreed to let it be that. (Whoever that small percentage is, it is not me.) If you want him home all the time and not working like that, how about you get a job and let me be a stay at home husband / boyfriend? Give me your debit card or money. Let me shop all day and take care of home. You can stay out late or whatever. I'll be here to give you sex whenever. I think men and women should switch certain shoes for a

week and see what it's like to be one another.

Chapter Seven

Being Water to Fire

Water is proven to be the only thing that can truly beat fire. It kills fire instantly. Yes, there have been big fires to where you need an excessive amount of water to put the fire out, but water will always win the battle. Gasoline, fuel, and other chemicals can ignite a fire. They can spread and feed the flame to make it dangerous. At that point, there is nothing that can stop it if no water is being used. Now, this can cause severe damage and can be fatal. What does water to fire mean to us as a couple, friends, or whatever we are? To me, this is an essential key to being in a successful relationship, especially if such a thing occurs. This is kind of like a branch off from nagging and attitudes, but it still deserves its own lane.

A lot of women can talk a lot of trash to a man when they know that he wouldn't do anything to them. Women can run off at the mouth and say the shadiest things. Not to mention the things that they do. But I must say, some men also do the same. But, we're talking about you and how you can keep me in ways by creating more security and being able to be my peace, the water to my fire. There are times when we have had a horrible day, and there are times where the smallest things can irk the hell out of us that probably wouldn't if it was a typical day. A lot of times, it has nothing to do with the woman in our life. There are times when I don't feel like being bothered at that particular moment because of some dumb shit that may have happened. Then there are times when you are the problem. Maybe it is your attitude and nagging, which is finally catching up with me.

Whatever it is, it's getting on my last nerves and in different ways. I show you where it's taking me and how mad I'm getting. I try to stay calm then walk away from it. But here you go talking shit, and I mean a lot of shit. Me being who I am, I try telling you, "Hey, listen. Let's talk later," or "Leave me be right now." Or maybe I ignore you and walk away and leave you standing there so that you can follow me and continue talking. At this moment, I am at the point of "SHUT THE FUCK UP! YOU'RE GETTING ON MY DAMN NERVES!" So, now you feel like turning it up. "Nigga, you shut the fuck up" or "Who the fuck you are talking to?". Now it's a full-blown argument back and forth. Not to mention the fire is growing bigger and bigger. There's no telling on where it's going to lead or how far it may get.

Why feed fuel to fire and cause it to get bigger while making it worse? Why are you following me or choosing not to let it go? Especially when I'm trying to step away from the moment to redeem myself even if I'm getting on you about something. I could be wrong, and it may be something small, but what if I'm in the right about it? I try to keep the peace. You don't have to bow down for anything, but why not be water to my fire? Put me out and bring me back down to earth. That's the best option. Especially if you know I'm dominant or if you feel I'll never let you win. I just think that you have to be the more level headed one to diffuse the problem. We can always talk about it once I'm calm or even a day or two later. Yes, it should be vice versa; if the shoe was on the other foot.

I don't think that letting me go to sleep still arguing is good. Sometimes you just have to make it as though I won, and I got the last word. Sometimes you have to do your homework, study, observe and make mental notes on what pisses me off. Ask yourself, "What could get him to that point?". That'll help you with the things that you should not do next time and things you should do to diffuse it.

There are elements to life, and sometimes we have to use those elements to advance through things that keep us blocked in. When you become water to his fire, you always win. You keep your strength and hold your composure. That is the greatest move. Well, one of the greatest moves because there are others also that could make a harder punch. You can do things like saying, "Baby, let's pray." No man can fight that unless he's pure evil. Another thing that can be talked about in this chapter is a word that can be super negative if acted upon.

Petty: a behavior characterized by an undue concern for trivial matters, especially in a small-minded or spiteful way, a form of revenge. (7)

Our generation of today takes the word petty in action and runs completely with it. Don't let the new trend of being petty mess up your relationship or damper it. Some things you just have to leave in the streets because doing something like being petty can become a regret. To me, being petty is a form of childishness. Indulging in and showing petty behavior can get you cursed the hell out. It is not worth it when you have a good man that you are trying to keep or make yours. If you have to play the game of pettiness, just make sure you do it when it's funny and all good vibes. Then it will mean no harm. It could become harmful if you use it when there is an argument or when bad things are happening. Remember to be the water to his fire.

Chapter Eight

Power of the Tongue

The tongue has the power to control life or death. The tongue can very well speak things into existence. That's what the Bible says in many chapters, and it's just written in different ways. Here we will speak on something that most of the world does that is not good at certain times and in certain situations.

Assumptions: a thing that is accepted as true or sure to happen,

without proof. (8)

Assumption can be the root cause of why some things happen. It can shake many things up in the bag. It can bring your imagination into existence. Bringing something that isn't real into reality. This something can be birth in a few different ways, such as:

- Insecurities

- Bad Conscious

- Low Self-esteem

- Fear

Just like the others, this word can be negative or positive. To me, it leans more towards negative because there is no need to assume when you can find out the answer. I do realize women have gone through a lot in life, especially when it comes down to men, which I will dig into later. Some women often make assumptions because of the flaws they see in themselves. This leads them to believe that no man can be trusted. They'll look around all of the beautifully built good-looking women and feel that it would be hard to keep who they have in their possession. This is also something I'm going to focus more on later.

They let their minds tell them that I am not really into her or that I am cheating on her. Her insecurities will have her feeling that the woman in the grocery store that appeared to have smiled at me is cheating with me. Though she may not speak on it now, she will hold it until she's ready to present her assumptions. It doesn't matter what it is. When her mind begins eating at her about something, she needs to change, or during any little argument, she will start to say slick things in reference to cheating or flirting.

Nowadays, women and men can get crazy with their assumptions. I must say women play no games with it, and it gets to a point where it becomes super sickening, just like with the nagging and the attitude. It makes us want to up and leave once the fussing and assuming starts. Don't get it twisted. Sometimes what you believe can be right. I will break the code one time. You may get the same reaction if you're right or wrong, but it's on you to know who you are involved with from the jump.

The point is when you're wrong, and it's just you tripping, you will probably get a calm "Babe stop it. You know I won't cheat on you," "You know I'm not cheating on you, nor am I flirting" or "I'm not interested in no one but you. Why are you assuming?" As it goes on, he will start becoming more sick of it and tired of being accused of things. Accusations like I'm sexing this one, messing with that one, and why is she looking at you. "I saw her throw an extra swing in her hips when she saw you in the mall." It just becomes plentiful.

You may even do it so badly to where I start saying hurtful things like "She's looking because I'm in great shape," — something like this can make her feel like I'm drowning her physical appearance. Or I may say, "Maybe she is trying to figure what I see in you,"; which I myself would never say, but it could be a thought. I could say something that doesn't hurt, but she may see it as me being a smart Alek like, "Maybe she is throwing her hips for you. How do you know she isn't into girls?"

Ok. Let's get to the point. The point is that the tongue has power. If you're going to keep assuming and standing by your assumptions, it is like ok I might as well do it. If you already have it in your head that I am, then that means I'm already at fault and found guilty of cheating. So, if I do it, you already knew I was, so that is a done deal now.

This can also be flipped because it can be that you're cheating, and your conscious is eating you up. Even still, there is still a bit of confusion as far as the assumption. How is it that once you found out that I did eventually cheat by force, you act all dramatic? You act super hurt as if you are in shock. Is it because you fed yourself a bunch of stuff that isn't real? Why feed yourself negative thoughts or continuously assume if you're not doing it to compare yourself mentally? You cry wolf so much to when, it happens, and you go mentally crazy. Tearing stuff up and keying cars. Is it worth it? If you don't have hardcore evidence or if you know that you are tripping, why act on it or even take a chance for it to become a reality? Why start breaking down a foundation that you've taken the time to build or a foundation that you're trying to develop?

Again, these are some of the keys to how to keep a black man. There's only so much a man can take. There's only but so much patience that a person can have with bullshit. It's just not something a man can tolerate for so long before he starts to lose his cool or walk away: a relationship filled with anxiety, self-doubt, insecurities, etcetera, It can be headed for pure hell, which leads me to the next chapter.

Chapter Nine

Self-Respect & Loving Yourself

Self-respect and loving yourself are essential if you want to be successful. To some men, this may not be very important, but to me, it is. Why is it important?

Self-Respect: Pride and confidence in oneself, a feeling that one is behaving with honor and dignity. (9)

Loving yourself: It's important to understand that you have to love yourself before you can love anyone else or before anyone can love you. (SD)

I believe a lot of you are either lost, or you just don't give a damn about yourself. Like ok, if you really sit back and analyze the things you've done, you could be in total disgust with yourself unless you've grown to change and be classier. Some of you are out there real heavy. Then you want someone like me to save you and sweep you off your feet. You would love me to make you wifey and the queen of my life. How could you honestly want that if you are still who you were years ago? Same ole' so and so from the block? When and where does it become a time to get a new start? Or when does this cycle come to a halt? Why is the answer always IDGAF? When life throws you a curveball to test your strength and faith, why do you run from it? Why is it IDGAF when someone points out those flaws? Why not change it or listen? Or maybe get help to become better.

You have to love yourself. It starts with having self-respect for who you are, where you are trying to go, and for what you want to do. I believe no man wants a woman that does not love herself. Well, a few types will feed off that and take advantage of those flaws. I do not want a woman that can't keep herself looking nice outside of work.

Hopefully, you look presentable at work. I don't want a woman that has terrible hygiene and just smells bad. I don't want a woman with her nails chewed up looking dirty with a torn up weave where I can see the tracks and glue crust caked up. Hair looking like fall season with all that dandruff flakes all over your hair. I mean, that is no self-respect and reads as you don't love yourself. Let's say even if times are hard, do something. Don't just start looking like a bum of a female. Now you find yourself letting two or three guys ride a train on you and slut you out because you want to try to fit in. You will end up doing many things that you are going to regret later if you do start to change.

You can get rid of a felony and sometimes a police record, but you can't erase your track record with sex partners and all of the wild things you've done. You can't get rid of the things that you do or did that made you be looked at or be seen as such a person. All you can do is make a drastic change to try to regain self-respect and try to come back to loving yourself. You have to get yourself together before you can do anything. It may not be the type of things that I've named. It could be you just need to work on trusting and loving. Those things can consist of assuming, bad attitudes, or stuff you know that has been horrible for your past relationships. This brings me to another big word that can be very positive in someone's life. The word is change.

Change: to make or become different. (10)

Change can be good or bad, depending on what kind of difference you are searching for. However, we are trying to speak positively in this part of the book. So anything that resembles negative is a NO. In order to start having both self-respect and the strength to love yourself, you would have to change who you are. Make your current you to who you once were. Many people are afraid of and fear change, especially if it's for the better. Change can involve several different things in your life. Of course, self or some of the other things could be scenery. Sometimes you need to change your surroundings before you become lost or end up just being a product of your environment. Being in the wrong place can play a significant part in who you are and who you eventually become. If you live in a drug-infested area, you may do drugs. If you hang around drug dealers, you may sell drugs, or you may just be a project chick.

Another thing that can play a major part in changing for the good is changing the people that are around you; friends or even family. They say you are who you hang with. If you hang with a bunch of females, yes, you are ratchet. If you hang with a lot of boosters, yes, you are a booster. If you hang with hoes, dirty females, shady people, liars, and so on, you will be looked at as one. The crazy thing about that is you may truly not be one of what they are, but since you affiliate yourself with them, then you may be labeled the same.

Yes, this is assuming, but the evidence is that all your friends are what they are. You could do things at the moment that could become a bad habit like club-hopping, smoking weed, or being on the block like one of the homies. So, of course, changing your habits is very important because a bad habit starts to become natural and then it becomes an everyday life for you.

Habit: a settled or regular tendency or practice, especially

that is hard to give up. (11)

If you do start or do something, make sure it is not a habit. That is the key unless it is a good habit. Again, everything can be positive or negative. How about getting into a habit of getting your hair done, nails done, washing your ass, going to work, paying your bills, saying no when you should, being too kind-hearted, etcetera. Sometimes you have to change the type of man that you go for. If you dated four dudes that you met in a club and neither of them had a job. Why keep going for the club type? If you dated a drug dealer or two and the police raided them, they're in and out of jail, the jack boys kicked in your house door and held you at gunpoint, and he's no way to be found, or even worse. Why keep going for that type? If you dated three street dudes and all three of them physically harmed you in some way. Why keep choosing that type?

I can go on and on, but why not get a nine-to-five guy? Why not get a churchy type? Why not get one who's trying to be something?

Why not give that same dude that you call a square a shot? Why do you keep settling for those other types? This all leads to self-respect and loving yourself. If you do not possess the two things, you will only be a puppet on a string or a pawn on a chessboard. You will just be a sacrifice. Another black woman that has been used. I don't need a dummy. I don't want someone that I can't trust because she can't trust herself. Therefore, you are not in my best interest if you don't respect yourself, and if you don't love yourself.

I believe that God is the ultimate judge over the world, but you will still be judged by your own actions. I say that to say this. If I meet you and I love who you are and know who you once were, then there is no problem. I will not judge you off your past because that was before me. Just say you tell me who you once were in your past to get it all out after a few weeks. That's cool, but if I like who you are today, with me, your past won't harm our future. If I meet you and you show a lot of bad habits and your messed up ways, then I would have no choice but to judge your past because obviously you are still stuck in your own ways. I can accept who you are as a person, along with your past.

If I really like you, I can learn your past and who you are and try to help change you for the better. However, you have to want to change.

Some women don't want to change or are just stuck in their own ways. They start to ask themselves questions. "Why do I have to change?" "Why can't I change?" It's because you are stuck in your past, and I want to try to get you out of it. I'm not saying that I am perfect, but I can say that I am on my 'ish as a man, which is probably why you want to be in a relationship with me in the first place.

You cannot fear change. Get past fear and make the best of yourself. If you like, love, and want to be with me, you will have no problem bettering yourself. Don't be like others and say to yourself, "If he doesn't like me for me, oh well," "Nothing is wrong with me," or "Maybe it's him that needs changing." You might even say, "I am who I am, and I'm not changing for anybody." Don't make excuses in order to trick yourself into thinking you are ok to everybody and say they are the ones that need to change. You have to ask yourself, "Why is he judging me or continuing trying to get me to change?"

Don't always take judging badly. It's just another word that can be used interchangeably negative or positive. Sometimes someone judging can help you want to change who you are. Change is not taking your name or inner self from you. It is just bringing out the best you possible. To answer your question on why I judge or ask you for change, it's because I like you, and the negative characteristics and behaviors are the only things holding you back from the blessing. I want to see the real you. The one that grew up wanting to be a nurse or work in criminal justice. I see so much potential in you.

If you can get out of your ways and let me upgrade you, you can be great. Set your pride aside. Just let go and allow the change. Don't be too proud to let someone hold your hand that probably actually cares about you. Don't run them away with talks of "I'm not changing for anybody." All of this is a part of loving yourself, loving yourself enough to better yourself. Don't be embarrassed and let your mind feel ashamed to show that yes, I do want to change, and yes, I do need help.

I remember when I was in school, and the teacher did some type of math problem. I couldn't understand it. I used to be like, "What?". She did it like two or three times and then asked the class if we understood. Everyone said yes, but I raised my hand and told her I don't get it. I knew I wasn't the only one that didn't understand it. There were most likely others that didn't either, but they didn't say anything because they didn't want to look dumb. On the other hand, I didn't care. I chose to raise my hand. Why? Because I wanted to understand. I wanted to learn because I didn't want to fail at anything.

I tried to put all that I have into everything that I did when it comes to surpassing the next level of education. I want to continue the process of upgrading my knowledge. This is the correct time not to care what no one thinks because only you can secure your future. When I was young, it was just bigger than facing my mother or facing an ass whooping if I failed school. It was about wanting to learn for myself because I respect myself enough to want to better myself. I never want to miss out on my blessings. I don't want to settle and be a could've been. I don't believe you, as a woman, should settle with the way that you are or the way you look if you have the power to change it.

Flaw: a mark, fault, or other imperfection that mars a

substance or object. (12)

To me, a flaw is something that you can change, but you chose not to. Some say a flaw is like things that you can't help as it's just you. However, you want to see it. I feel people create their shortcomings. They do nothing to change them now and that's why they become flawed. You leave those flaws unattended to for so long that it becomes a part of who you are for good. Now that this unhealthy flaw has become a regular habit, it comes to a point where you cannot change them even if you wanted to. These things are holding you down like burdens and anchors, making you sink as if you were in a bathtub. Get yourself together, and do not be content. Don't settle. Change whatever you can to make you feel better and to make you better. Love yourself, gain some self-respect, and be the best person that you can be.

Chapter Ten

Sacrificing

It seems that sacrificing is almost impossible with my beautiful black woman. This is as bad as wanting her to change some of her bad habits and ways. This world has things lopsided when it comes to a man and a black woman. Why is it that I have to sacrifice so much to make you happy and make things happen? Why is it that when the table is turned, it is a problem? Let me hop into the topic and point out some things, or the difference between when a black man sacrifices and when a black woman sacrifices.

Ok, now I meet a woman who lives maybe 35 minutes away from where I live. She invites me to her house, which is cool. It turns out to be fun and a good idea. We realized how cool one another is, so now it's nothing to be able to go to her house. In fact, she starts to love spending time with me. It got to where I was coming over to her house after working two jobs. Even if it was for a few hours by her request to see me. As times passed, it began to wear and tear on my body from working long hours at work. It was ok until one day when I considered what could be a solution to avoid things being one-sided.

"Sweetheart, do you think you can you come over to my place?" It made more sense since she only worked one job. She even had days off. There should not have been a problem. WRONG!!!! She would say she's too tired or did not feel like driving. Instead, she would tell me, "Babe, can you just come here" with no care that I've been coming for two months straight, losing sleep, falling asleep coming to her house, almost wrecking, and losing my life period. I had been going over to her house to have sex and fall asleep only to wake up three hours before work. NO SACRIFICE!

One of the biggest things some women do not want to sacrifice is true quality time. Women can't give up or sacrifice social media or their cell phones. I don't care what's going on, other than during sex, she is going to look at her phone and go on social media. Social media is more important than life sometimes. It seems like social media is pure evil. It is one of the assassins that can quickly bring death to a relationship. Since we are discussing social media, let's jump off the subject for a second to touch on that in-depth.

Social media is proven to break up happy homes and relationships. Here are some examples. Someone may love your post too much and make crazy comments that you can't control. It maybe someone you may or may not know or a person that you are trying to get to know as a friend. You can be completely innocent, but social media can still make you look like a terrible lying, cheating, and no good ass person. Anyone in the world could go on your Facebook, click on messages, and call or video chat you. You can delete or even block them, but all they have to do is create another page and do it all over again. That alone could cause some serious issues. In fact, issues that could get very dangerous.

People can comment about whatever they feel on your page or post whatever they think, and that alone can cause serious harm to someone's relationship. Someone can tag you on his or her page on a post saying whatever they like. That can also cause severe damage. People are randomly sending you DMs that consist of all types of different things; perverted messages and sexually explicit pictures. You may not have a clue as to why, but again that can cause critical issues to your relationship. People don't realize the dangers to it all, but there is a level to these things also. It may not seem fair, but it's real.

When dating someone in the music industry, you can only expect for these types of things to take place. This can also happen if you are a model, actor, or a host and in similar industries. However, if you're just a manager at Wal-Mart, there is no excuse for these situations. He or she has to have a following of fans, supporters, and a huge social media presence. If one of you is in the industry, you have to interact and entertain the fans. It is not good if your partner is insecure or jealous. Therefore, it's probably best that you do not date a person in the industry if you have these traits.

Nevertheless, by you working at Wal-Mart, you shouldn't have all of that going on your social media. This unacceptable on your end because you don't have an image to keep up with or fans to entertain. But if this is happening to you, it could be a problem if it is happening on your social media.

Social media could have the person that you are dating, thinking it's impossible for you to go without being on it. It can become a huge problem to where it's like, "Damn, you come over here, and you are just going to be on your social media? You could've stayed at home?" Or it could have you saying, "Damn, can I get some attention?", "I hope you sleep well with your phone tonight" or "Just call one of your friends that you are messaging and poking all day."

Now, I have seen couples share Facebook pages, but I think that when you are in the industry, it wouldn't be a good idea. At least until you're in the industry and established, I think if you controlled yourself more with discipline, especially when it comes to Bae time, it wouldn't be so bad looking because it will be more respectful. However, if you do it anytime during Bae time, it would be viewed as total disrespect unless that person is doing it or has done it as well. Nevertheless, I know there are times where a person will hop on their social media just because the other person is on their social media. So, the best thing to do is just cut it out or at least discipline it more.

I am going back to the topic at hand, sacrificing. In all actuality, we never left that topic because that was a lesson of sacrifice when we spoke about social media. I believe in treating people how you would like to be treated. There shouldn't be anything one-sided. It's only right that you match the other person's sacrifice. I call this being a mirror. It is the action of mirroring whoever is in your circle. It means giving them what they give you; action for action. So, when you're happy, that means I'm happy. When you're sad, that means I am sad.

Anytime that you are not happy, I probably won't be either. Do you know what it truly means? It means that it's you. You are causing the stir of events or reactions that come from me. So basically, you are looking at yourself in the mirror when you look at me. You're not feeling the way I've been acting. You say that I've changed. You say that I stay in my feelings, and you express that you are not down with that bullshit. Well, you need to be getting yourself together because baby, I'm just giving you the same energy I'm receiving from you. So now, you know how it feels. What it feels like to be with you. If you keep it right and stay one way, it will work out. If not, it won't. Sometimes you have to sacrifice to make things work out. Remember, sacrifice doesn't always mean negative.

Sacrifice: an act of giving up something valued for the sake of something else regarded as more important or worthy. (13)

If you can't sacrifice for me, maybe I am not as important as you claim I am. Especially if it is something that's not more important than happiness. I believe things are so crazy in the world that when we hear certain words, it is automatically looked at as a bad or negative thing. Just like the word CHANGE. It is looked at like someone is talking down on you or like they just feel that they are better than you are. Sometimes we have to look outside the box and look at the positivity it can breathe into your life. Sometimes people can be better at helping others than helping themselves. Maybe building you up can roll back on to me. If I can make you better, then perhaps you can come and give back to me so that I can become great like you. Don't miss your blessing because you feel you're good as you are or because you think that you shouldn't have to sacrifice. Everything that I spoke on previously falls under the word sacrifice. That, to me, is very important—SACRIFICE!

Chapter Eleven

A Man's Worth
Vs.
A Woman's Worth

The Importance of A Woman

This chapter is going to be very deep. It will probably cause an uproar. What is about to be talked about is very real and needs to be known. People might have talked about this somewhere in the world, but I think it needs to be spotlighted again and more in-depth. The difference and comparison between the two sexes will blow your mind. So maybe we should just hop into it.

Ladies, why are you so important to the world? What makes you different? A woman can birth life. She has the ability to form a human being inside of her. She keeps the world full of human life. However, while it doesn't make you overall valuable, it does make you significant to the world. The reason that you aren't the most important is that the only woman that has woken up pregnant is the Virgin Mary. Therefore, you can't give life nor create it. Just as much as you're carrying a human life the man carries thousands of them. Yes, you can go lesbian. But at the end of the day, you still need men for creating life whether you go to a donor, you adopt, or if you have sex with him. What can you possibly do? I bet it wouldn't work if you tried injecting a woman's juices in you.

A woman thinks better with some things. She is more levelheaded than a man is. Women are needed more than a man is with certain stuff. For instance, a woman can get a toy—a dildo or vibrator— and will be pleased. If she deals with another woman, it is viewed differently than a man messing with another man. See, a man isn't into any toys and most are not with the homosexual situation. Therefore, it is more painful for the guy to be without the woman. So, yes, she is more important in that area.

Women are very caring, passionate, and more mature. Or let's just say she matures faster than a lot of men. A woman can have a baby at 15, 16, or 17 years old and love it naturally before she's ever experienced raising or caring for a child. Men do not possess that part of the mind. We would be lost if we had to raise a child at that age. Women are the backbones of the family. They hold things together. Most are more responsible than some men can ever be when it comes to responsibilities such as bills getting paid. Whereas some men will mess up the money and put themselves in a hole.

Proverbs 31:10-12 (NKJV)

"Who can find a virtuous wife?

For her worth is far above rubies.

The heart of her husband safely trusts her;

So he will have no lack of gain.

She does him good and not evil all the days of her life."

Proverbs 31: 14-18 (NKJV)

"She is like the merchant ships,

She brings her food from afar. She also rises while it is yet night,

And provides food for her household,

And a portion for her maidservants.

She considers a field and buys it.

From her profits she plants a vineyard.

She girds herself with strength,

And strengthens her arms.

She perceives that her merchandise is good,

And her lamp does not go out by night."

Proverbs 31:21 (NKJV)

"She is not afraid of snow for her household,

For all her household is clothed with scarlet."

Proverbs 31:25-28, 31 (NKJV)

"Strength and honor are her clothing;

She shall rejoice in time to come.

She opens her mouth with wisdom,

And on her tongue is the law of kindness.

She watches over the ways of her household,

And does not eat the bread of idleness.

Her children rise up and call her blessed;

Her husband also, and he praises her:

Give her of the fruit of her hands,

And let her own works praise her in the gates."

The scriptures above help to prove your importance and worth to us as men. Ladies, you would die for your kids. You would give them your all. You love harder than we could. It runs deep. Sometimes it's so deep that it could make you crazy. I've seen the most insane chain of events when it comes from your love and your heart for a man. Granted, it's not always bad. Sometimes it's good things that make you do so much. Just as much as your daughter needs you, that little boy needs you as well.

I know that I will get a lot from what I'm about to say, but I think women teach boys to be men better than a man can with certain things. It's essential to have a woman's touch on things. Without it there's a big void that cannot be filled. She's the glue that holds things together. She's the levelheaded one that keeps things from going left on the outside. She is his other half and his ride or die. She's there when no one else is. She is Tasha to Ghost. She is Jada to Will. She is Bonnie to Clyde. And when all else fails, if she's the woman she's supposed to be, you can't lose. Nothing or no one can break this bond. The only way it can be broken is if one of you breaks it. When things are crazy and you need uplifting, she will be your best motivator you could ever have. She'll give you the best prep talk to lift you better than any of your homeboys could ever give.

The Importance of A Man

Now, let's talk about the importance of a man. Talking about this is going to be a little deeper because the things that I'm going to talk about are always overlooked. We don't receive enough appreciation for it. Where do I start? Let's start on the regular stuff and then we'll talk about that deep stuff.

Men are important because we are providers. We take most of the pressure of making sure the more important things are handled. We make life easier when we are in the picture. When it comes to things like bills for an example. We have the responsibility for rent, lights, cars, and sometimes insurance. It's like it is normal for a man to go broke and without to take care of these things, while the woman only has to worry about the simple little bills. If we are not in the picture, hopefully she has either her mom or her dad to help. Alternatively, she could be on section 8 or she could be living alone trying to figure out when the bills are going to stop, thinking to herself, "I need to get a job, I got to get a man, and I can't do this." It might get as bad as her feeling as if she should get a sugar daddy because she was taught it's easier with a man because she could just use his money.

The furthest thing on her mind is using her own money or finding someone to go half-and-half with her. The man is actually rich. Even when you complain about him being a broke motherfucker. He can have absolutely nothing to his name and it still equals the importance of the man with all the money. Now, I got your attention. You want to know how, huh? Well, I'll explain how that same broke motherfucker as you put it is really rich.

Let's say you already have two kids when you meet him. Now, he probably doesn't have any kids. He may have a part-time job, makes less, or has a side job; that broke motherfucker is still rich. You ask yourself what if he has neither. Why are you still with this broke motherfucker? Ok, let's break it down. He's probably watching your kids while you're at work or out every day. So now, you don't have to take them to daycare. Guess what? He just saved you $750 per month and that's if you find a daycare that is $125 per child. So, that is money you now do not have to worry about paying. Ok, your car needs an oil change or something needs to be fixed.

Guess what? You're in luck because that broke motherfucker knows how to do it. Oh, remember you got that new Mercedes that you've always wanted? Well, the oil change on that car costs around $200. He's probably going to do it for $60, but that $60 is for the oil and filter to give you an oil change. However, let's not forget something else is wrong with the car. He fixes the problem. A problem that may cost you $250 if you go to a dealer or mechanic. He gets it done for you for only $100, which is basically for parts because the labor is free.

So he just saved you $290, when you could've paid out $450. That broke motherfucker is rich. Let's say you have a massive tree in your yard that started slanting into your neighbor's yard and it needs to be cut down. The lowest estimate that you got was $350 to have someone come out and perform the job. On top of that, you need the grass cut twice a month that costs $75 for both times and that's an extra $150. Well, guess what? He knows how to do both and probably borrows the equipment to get it done. He just saved you $500 and two more bills you don't have to worry about. He can cook, fix things, and he can clean all down to the gutters.

He helps the kids with their homework, teaches them how to fight, and washes the car. This broke motherfucker even does laundry, tire change, tune-ups. Shit, he might even grease your scalp or he might also help take your hair out. He lays good dick, eats good pussy, and rubs your feet. He might even learn how to do pedicures, give you a massage, read to your badass kids, get them together for school in the morning, and drive or walk them to school in the morning.

This broke motherfucker is actually rich. He's saving you a lot of money. He's saving you more money than a man that is putting money in your hands. All of these things cost a lot of money. So, while you are calling him a broke motherfucker, you're the one that's actually misleading because he's actually rich. Stop overlooking a man's importance because he may be less fortunate than other men. You never know you might get lucky. Shit, he may still do all of those things and even have a hell of a job.

We can do things that your body couldn't withstand doing because of the strength that we physically possess. If we were stranded in the middle of nowhere, we could probably get out and go get help with just the will power that we possess. We could carry you if we have to for a long distance. We can build and tear down. We can run a country and of course be huge providers. Just as much as you as women are needed in our life, men are also required.

We, as men, are born as natural leaders made to lead. You, as women, are made to keep things in order. You are like the vice president behind us. In no way, shape, or form am I talking down on you. However, didn't Jesus come as a man and weren't the most important people through time men; Moses, Sampson, Job, Abraham, David, Elijah, Isaiah, Noah, Peter, Paul, as well as many more.

Women tend to make men feel like they are not relevant or as if women are more important. However, we are just as important as a woman. Why do you think there were Adam and Eve; the first two people in the world? From them came everyone who has ever lived. However, it gets more in-depth than just these things because I speak on why men are more important. But, at the same time, showing is kind of more important in a sense also. Yes, I know it's confusing, but you have to look at it through your third eye and not just the two you use every day. Ok, so what are men considered other than a provider? A protector.

Protector: a person or thing that protects

someone or something. (14)

Do you realize that men are technically here for the disposal of women and the children only? What does that mean, you ask? Think about it. We are protectors. That means we are supposed to die for women. Let's leave out kids because the mother will die for the kids as well if need be. Even still, the man overall will die for all before the mother. Now let's say two or three guys break in your home. While they are there in the house, the first thing she's going to expect is for me to go out there and protect her. Which could lead to me killing somebody, beating the hell out of somebody or even worse vice versa. Let's not take this the wrong way. I am not, by any means, saying anything is wrong with the man being obligated to do so. He is supposed to. We are the Kings of the jungle. It's our duty to protect. It's also expected of him to die so the woman and the kids can live. Or if there are no kids, it may be meant for the woman to live.

She is going to expect the man to protect her by all means. Even if it means putting him in the crossfire to do so. Here are a few examples. Let's say y'all are out and someone starts shooting. The first thing she will do is get behind the man. Using him as a shield to save herself from bullets to ensure she does not get hit. I've known women that are drama queens and every time you look up she's in some type of drama.

The crazy thing is a lot of the times it was her mouth that kept her in stuff. In a lot of those situations, she would throw you inside the fire by telling people that she was going to put her dude on them. I found myself beefing with ghosts. These are people that I've never seen a day in my life. Now, I have to fight or have a shootout because of people that she is beefing with. Who are probably pure goons and don't give a damn about who or whatever. Again, she throws the man out there to be the protector or more so he's like her Pit bull than her man.

Now, I will automatically die for my kids if I have to without hesitation. A real man would anyway. You do have some people that are too selfish to leave or to die; like a kid. There is a rare breed of women who would try to think of a way before sending you in harm's way because she doesn't want you to die. Nor does she want harm towards you. She just wants it all to be a bad dream that we can wake up from.

As I said earlier, men are here to be a sacrifice and disposed of. Our purpose is to make sure women are protected and that they survive everything. This can mean three things: men are more important than women, a woman is more important than man, or we both have separate importance. To explain things further, if men don't die and protect women, then there would be fewer women. Which leads to fewer lives being born unto the earth.

This explanation seems to make sense, but it leaves us with this one question. If the blood of a man protects women, can the world still go on reproducing? I just realized that it actually would. If you think about it, why do you think there are many sperm banks? Some of these banks pay for sperm. So guess what, if we die, they can just inject women with the sperm that they have so much of and most likely those women will birth more men.

Therefore, I think women need to show more love and appreciation to a good man like myself because you do have an abundance of men that won't die at all. In fact, he would use you as a shield if it came down to it. Your responsibilities are nowhere as deep as ours are. You don't hear many stories of a woman being the protector. Don't get it misconstrued, though. Some ride or die and will ride with us. Like if I fight, we both fight. She says things like, "Bae, I am not about to sit back and watch you get jumped. That ain't happening."

I think there is a small group of women that will step in front of a gun to protect her man. So, yes, I take that back. Five percent of women want to protect or help prevent a man from getting hurt.

However, as I said before, a woman will be at disposal for her kids. You can trust and believe that. They would rarely have to if a man is present. So, when you say, "A man isn't worth shit," please rethink that statement. He is rich, he is a provider, he is a protector, and if he can do all the things that are named here in the chapter he is a true guardian. He is like Heimdall, Idris Alba, Thor: The Guardian.

Chapter Twelve

Knowing When He's Ready to Walk

Like a woman, a man has a boiling point. A point till there's times to call it quits. The only difference is that women are more forgiving and can take a lot more than men can ever take. I mean a woman can go through the cheating phase. They can even go through physical and mental abuse. I believe and kind of understand how and why they do it. I can't say any of it is a positive, but I kind of see how it is almost a positive thing for them.

There is such a thing as her loving too hard. Something that can blind you from the truth in that particular situation. Love overpowers the mind and controls the situation if your mind is strong enough to overthink at that time. It can be because she doesn't want to be without that man. She always dreamed and has faith that they will always be with each other for the rest of their lives. And for her, it's like whatever it is that they are going through can be worked out and overcome.

She is so used to him being there and she knows he handles responsibilities at home. He could be a good man but just has some shitty habits or messed up ways about himself. It also can be that she doesn't want everybody and their mama to know that everything in her perfect little world isn't perfect to the people looking in. It can also be because she is afraid and she doesn't know what he may do if she calls it quits or walks away. Therefore, she has to plan and have perfect timing to safely get away from a situation that she is in with that person.

In this case, it could be dangerous for either one of them because it can get too crazy. She'll just do what she has to do to make it happen. Especially, if she decides to tell him, but he aggressively tells her "It ain't over until I say it's over." Now, that's where it gets crazy. From a man's side of it, it's just straight-up "Look, I'm done; with no ifs, ands, or buts about it." A woman can cheat and do something crazy one time, and it'll be over between the two. She'll become every name in the book.

Ladies, here are a few clues to tell when he's preparing to walk away from what y'all have. If sex slows down drastically and he becomes distant with it. Yes, it can mean that he's losing that physical connection with you. If you're talking to him sexually, he's not even responding as he usually does and it becomes a pattern. It could mean that he is losing interest. It can mean that he's starting to lose all desire to sexually talk to you. It's as if he is disgusted by it. If you tell him that you love him, get a little sensitive and mushy with him and he doesn't react and it becomes a pattern, maybe he's losing that emotional connection with you. At this point, it's not looking too good with him being happy with you.

Even when you do have sex, you can feel he's not into it and he is absent to what you two always called good loving. Further signs of trouble can be if he starts to stay out all night and stops caring about you tripping, or if he starts sleeping a good distance from you in the bed. He may begin to stop allowing things to get to him when he usually would've given you pure hell about it. Now yes, he could be saying to himself, "I'm not going to let her bother me anymore." He makes changes, but it could also mean that he is on his last leg with you and the drama. If y'all really talk and the communication starts to be little to none, it is coming to an end. Men are so easily thrown off by shit that he's not down with a relationship. Now, don't get it twisted. Some of us will try a little harder to make shit work because we actually care and may want to be with you.

However, it seems like sometimes the more we try the more pointless it becomes. Women can't just say it's always our fault why the relationship didn't or isn't working. Women need to take accountability as well. It is y'all just as much as it is us. Sadly, women will still point the blame because they hate looking to be at fault or to look bad in front of people. Men have and will continue to be a woman's punching bag. We have to carry the fault, blame, hard times, tears, slander, and even be guilty of most things.

We just can't win. It's bad enough we're black and have to deal with society. We're fighting every day to stay alive in the hood with all these haters and the predators of the streets. We have to fight the police every day because we might pass through the hood or because we fit the description of someone; look suspicious, or drive a nice car. We work hard to be able to buy what we want but are still suspect of society. Hell, it's even worse if you decide to date a white woman because it would be looked at as if we forced them to be in a relationship with us.

Fighting to get through every police encounter. Not knowing that if we grab our license, registration or car insurance, we might get shot down or beaten to death. Then we're at work putting up with bullshit with our boss, co-workers, and customers every day. It just seems like everybody is just taking us through unnecessary bullshit. So, for us to come home and deal with some more bullshit we don't need that in our lives. It is unnecessary.

As I said in a few chapters back, we just want peace. We want to escape the bullshit that we have to go through every day. What y'all have to understand is that we have to bite our tongues in those situations; at our jobs and with police encounters as such. We try to hold our tongue with you too. I'm sorry to say it's more free will when it comes to you because in that situation he's the King of the jungle. So y'all get the worst of it. Even when it's not really meant for y'all. He's so fed up that he decides to say, "Look, I'm out." It's not just that moment or day that did it. It's all the shit from before that has built up that he didn't really trip about at that time.

When things like this occur, often where he starts to spaz out on you about something you say things like, "Why you ain't tell your boss or the people in the streets the same thing that you are telling me? Why didn't you check them?" What you fail to realize is that he wants to go off on their ass just as much. He can't because those situations are different. One writes his checks so that those bills can get paid. The police can arrest, beat him down, or kill him if they feel any harm.

There are levels to this. If he goes to your family, like your sister or mother, to try to get answers as to why you are the way you are it means that he is trying. It is becoming a lot for him. This situation is becoming an anchor. You will definitely be upset if he goes to your family because you know how they'll start looking at you. If you look at it in a different light, you can at least say he cares enough to try to understand you before ultimately deciding to give up on you.

Now, mind you, this is after him trying to get you to communicate and tighten up. Which may never happen. It's like a parent that has to keep repeating themselves about something, but the child just keeps on doing it. There will become consequences for having to keep telling them repeatedly. It's the same with relationships. It just becomes more permanent on what is done and said. At this point in a relationship, it is just done.

What you ladies have to know and realize is that sex is not always the answer to solving issues. You can't always think that giving me some head or pussy, which is probably amazing, will get him to stay. Most of the time, change and communication are the answers because obviously whatever it is you're doing wrong you can change. Waiting until it's too late, which is the same as last-minute situations, is definitely not the answer. I think that once a woman stops being selfish and realizes that it's not always about them and they learn to accept the importance of a man and how much the man brings to the table, then it'll result in better outcomes.

If I'm in a relationship, where I feel less than a man or feel like I mean nothing and that she is more important than myself, I have to go. If I feel like I have to go through hell and high waters to keep her, all just to make her happy and to take care of her just for me to go without, I'm out. If I have to fight to keep her every single time there is a small issue and she wants to leave every single time, I'm out. I have experienced every other day breakups over nothing at all. I have been with women that feel that the world revolves around them and if it doesn't she's out.

To women, men should have no feelings outside of worshiping the grounds she walks on. The minute that a man starts to feel some type of way about things it is perceived that we're acting like a punk; we're soft and we should man-up, stop acting sensitive, and so on. Y'all feel that a man is supposed to be pain proof. We are supposed to be like programmed robots under the orders of a woman. Now, at some point in time, it used to be like that and maybe some guys are still like that, but a lot of us smartened up.

I bring too much to the table to be anything less than a man. I will not take anything less than what I deserve. I understand my importance, worth, how I change and control lives with my obligation men have been defaulted to be and to do. Therefore, I will only accept a woman that understands these things and feels appreciated that I'm in her life. I will free myself of anything less. Once I am gone I will not entertain coming back. Then you will experience knowing what you had and now it's gone.

Yes, I said knowing instead of not knowing what you had until it's gone. I used knowing because you're going to know what you're gonna have the way I walked into your life. Not knowing means I never showed myself to you. It means I held back. So, that would mean it was a losing battle for you from the jump. I will show you what you have in hopes that you do what's right to keep it forever. Hopefully, you take heed and better your relationship. Even if you think that there's nothing wrong make sure.

Don't be afraid to change for better, not worse. Don't be scared to want to do more and keep the spice. It keeps the fire burning. Don't be feeling yourself so much to you think I'm supposed to have you walking around on rose petals while I walk through mud. Don't leave the door open for another woman to be able to show him what he's worth and what he should be getting.

Extra Info

I went out and asked a few people their thoughts on keeping a professional black man and what can make him not want to stay? We're going to get into some real opinions from real people. Nothing is made up. Some responses are positive and show growth among black women and some remain the same exactly as before; selfish with no hint of growth. Some of them will be mad even though I've decided not to insert names because of what I am about to say. Again, all are real people and none are fictionalized. I will comment my opinion on each.

Unknown Female #1

"I truly believe a man has to want to be in a relationship to be kept. He has to want you with his heart, mind, body, and soul. If a man feels unappreciated, he won't stay, especially if he's doing his best by you." For me, the question wasn't fully answered. It's a bit more on the side of what he has to do versus what she has to do and what she thinks can push him away. Therefore, I rate this under a little selfish in my eyes.

Unknown Female #2

"I think what keeps a man is loyalty is someone who appreciates his profession and wants to help him grow. If she's holding him down, complaining about his profession and how she's not satisfied because he's always working and trying to better himself, that would definitely make him seek other women. If you both can't appreciate and grow together what's the point?" This response clearly answered the question. It explained what she thought it took to keep a professional black man and what could make him walk. This is a good message to insert into what you believe yourself.

Unknown Male

"She has to have understanding. She has to realize that they're going to be late nights and a lot of people who are going to want to talk and interact; especially women. But it is just business. She has to realize that I'm not cheating or doing anything wrong and understand that what we do is not a 9 to 5 job with a paycheck every week. There may be rough moments money wise, but we'll make it work." I gotta agree that it's only right for her to understand this part of the game. Not every man is a cheater or wishes to cheat. Not every man is easily influenced into doing things that they shouldn't. Do not let insecurities get the best of you in my career. Everything is business. Yeah, money can be crazy sometimes, but that is a part of the come up. It just makes me hungrier to want to eat.

Unknown Female #3

"Men do not want a woman who complains and nags all of the time. I've learned that a long time ago that can ruin a relationship. Loyalty is everything to a man, never mess that up, or he's definitely gone. I don't care what happens. Your loyalty will first and foremost be with your man. A man doesn't want a lazy woman. Even if they have all the money in the world to afford maids or housekeepers, etc. He needs to know that if hard times come, you will be able to perform those duties."

There goes loyalty again. Loyalty is something a man loves to hear and knows that is a part of the relationship. A woman that hasn't been in relationships and is currently in her first one or trying to be in one should take all of this in. Only a mature, grown, changing woman can admit her faults and learn from them; not just blame men and make them out to be at fault all the time. That's a special type of woman. She's going to be the one to get that ring and have him for life.

Unknown Woman #4

"I honestly don't think there is a certain thing you have to do to keep a man. He has to want to be kept. Y'all have to be meant for each other. I feel, if a man truly loves you, he won't do anything to lose you and vice versa. A woman can make him feel less of a man even though he's really focused on trying to do the right thing and accomplish goals. But all she does is bring up the negative and isn't encouraging or she is not there to listen when he needs to talk."

For me, the second response is more on point with the answer for what will make him leave. That first answer though is just something that screams selfish also. I noticed asking women these questions 87% brought the issue back around to incorporate themselves. She didn't really answer the question. It was basically saying me, me, me, and not about the topic at hand. What do you think it takes to keep a professional black man? Others answered it telling us what it would take to keep a professional black man. While she and the others answered it by saying he'll do what it takes not to LOSE ME if he genuinely wants to be with me. I'm like that is not the question. Ladies, you have to learn not to put yourself in front of everything. Sometimes it's about us, too. Don't be so self-centered to the point he doesn't matter or feel as such. Trust me. It is not something that he would deal with.

Keepin' a Thug Hustler

What's poppin', ladies? We ain't even gonna play. We're going in off top. I can't lie. I like shit a certain way, but I mean it's all good when it comes to certain shit too. I hear you wanna know what it takes to keep me. Shit, I'll share some knowledge on dat. I ain't trippin'. It's all good. So we're going to keep this introduction short and just start.

Chapter Thirteen

How I Was Raised
Who Am I?

I came into the world like everyone else through the vagina, but I was a product of my environment. Meaning I did not grow to be a pussy. I was born to be a thug. I skipped normal childhood. Instead, I became a product of my environment where we live or where I was from. I came up under a family of hustlers and thugs from my mother down to my grandma.

Thug: a violent person, especially a criminal. (15)

Hustler: An aggressively enterprising person; a go-getter. (16)

Some would say I had it bad because I was a mixed breed—a thug and a hustler. I only get violent if it's called for. I didn't just go around beating up on people and don't look at myself as a criminal. I feel like I had to get through just like everybody else. Hell, if I'm a criminal, then that means most of our presidents and law enforcement are criminals too. When I was young, I found out that I had a gift of stealing, but before you judge me, I stole from the rich. Shit, to me, it wasn't fair. They were born without having to go through the struggle. If everybody did, the world would be different; a lot less judgmental, and racist.

Back in the day they called us hoodlums, street punks, or of course, thugs. I guess I fell under that thug category because that's all I heard. Don't get it twisted. Some of my uncles, peers, and OG's were more thug than I was because they weren't mixed. They were pure thugs. So what, they were violent. Shit, they didn't care who they were putting hands on. Most encounters with them would end up beating somebody up or catching an assault charge.

Nevertheless, I can get cutthroat if I need to. There have been times in my life where I had to bring it out. I did everything from breaking and entering, stealing, selling drugs, and straight robbing people. I grew up thinking this was who I truly was. I was robbing all the ones that were rich and throwing it up in the people's faces that had nothing. I hated that. I guess I'm a hater too. I fell deep into robbing. Soon after that, I slowly fell into the character of a thug more and more. Especially, when I started seeing how women started falling deep for my kind. Lord, I can't lie. Some of y'all are Tootoo.

TooToo : depending on how it is expressed it can be good or bad. In this case, it means fine as fuck without saying it, like "Damn, shawty Tootoo." (SD)

I believe any woman that sees or hears about me and still wants to be close to me is a keeper. It tells me that she's down or can be down for me. She's attracted to the thrill of the type of life I live every day. She knows what I'm capable of, but it's something that draws her to me more and more. She doesn't mind my pants sagging, get it by any means, crazy when I want to be, and street running ass. She allows me to be me. It turns her on the way I talk, walk, and my persona.

The more and more she's around me she starts to adapt to me. She may not just become my girl, but she is also my homie. I can pass her a blunt of loud and we can smoke and trip. She becomes someone that I can trust before I can with anybody in the streets. Those dudes in the hood like myself they're cutthroat. They get it by any means too. Together we are like a female that just brought her some Gucci and just got her hair done. So, my trust for her goes up more towards her because I can feel her vibes and how she moves.

There is no question on who I am and what I do. Shit, who doesn't know? We came up under the watch of Tupac; the inventor of thug life. Shit, thugs period. How do you feel about Tupac? We are always looked at as negative. We are that type that comes from struggle and poverty. We were told out the gate that we would end up dead or in jail. No one has, have, or had faith in us emerging from the slums. The system is designed to keep us on the ground with their foot on our necks. Imagine being born into a country of hatred from slavery to us getting shot down, life in prison (just for a little bit of drugs and no violence), having to sign a gun act with no violence on our record, and even having a gun on us period.

Meanwhile, when you go to the hood you see people with ARs, Uzis, and grenades as if a big ass case of guns was dropped in the hood or something. It doesn't matter what type of black man you are. The law still ends up giving two for one. Let's say I killed somebody. They'll give me life. That means two black men for the price of one. This is how we're raised trying to survive. You could be a regular black man and still get stereotyped and have bad encounters. This is how we have to come up.

Chapter Fourteen

Thug Loving-Sex

After learning about me and figuring out who I am and who I've become, she still falls for my type. She says I treat her differently from anybody else she's ever dealt with. Fa real, I don't know what it is she sees, but I just keep it 1000. Don't tell her everything, though, because the less she knows it's safe for us both. For now, I still let her in the moment that I'm living in. When I have a conversation with a woman I'm seeing, about what I'm dealing with on that level, I just give her the raw and uncut. I cannot give you sensitivity because I'm not that type. I give to you the only way I know how and that's straight to the point. I don't have time to be playing around.

So yea, my speech is aggressive, but that's just how I talk. I don't always mean verbal harm, but it is what it is, though. I'm just saying.

Let's talk about sex with me and what I like; the juicy part of this chapter. Who I am in the streets comes out during sex with me. Like I'm gonna leave my Timbs, chain, and gun on the dresser because I never can be too comfortable. I like it when you come out of the bathroom with some heels on, some thongs, and no bra at all, smelling all fruity and shit. DAMN! I can't lie. I love that whole turn on the music and dance for me shit, fa real. I'm a boss, so I want all that treatment.

I like that lap dance, twerking, stroking, touching, and all dat. I can't lie. The first thing after that, I need kissing all the way down to the D and shit. That turns me on automatic. I love to look down and see me all up in your mouth and you're looking up while you do it. If you're not doing that and you act like you don't, I'm cool on you fa real. I mean, I'll smash but nothing else. That's something that has to be done and should be done with no questions asked. FACTS!!! Then from there, I'm climbing in.

I'm not too much on eatin' that box. You might find a few. I mean, I might though. It depends on how good you were when you were down there. Like I said, you can expect me to rough you up, all that flipping and turning, and bouncing everywhere. When I get you from the back with my boots on to give me stability you're in trouble. I'm going deep. You can believe that—BIG FACTS!

I'm not good with that love making shit. I'm trying to pound on you again, fa real, since you like this thug life shit so much. You're always telling your friends how the shit turns you on so much. I know 80 percent of woman likes rough sex, maybe not all the time but often. So, be mindful when you're talking a good game because when I get a hold of you don't back down or get scared. Like Young Buck said, "You say you want a thug. Don't be scared now." So, since you want that thug loving, take that shit.

Once we crank up, you gotta make it through. No tapping out. You're about to get that pain, pleasure dick, that take yo ass to sleep dick, dat why you playin' with my dick. When I'm on top, I like to throw them legs up, stroke at the same time, and suck up on nipples. I mean, sex with me is off the chain and I'm very random and crazy. I'm just into doing crazy ass shit. Like what you ask? I might ask for some at the movie theater all the way to a dressing room in a clothing store. I'm a daredevil. I might be on the passenger side and say some shit like, "Bae, put the car on cruise control, let's see if I can steer, and you can give me some head."

Yes, ladies, call me crazy I bet you'll try or think about it. I might want it right after you've worked out. Yeah, I'm nasty. Give me that natural smell shit. I might even say let's do it on the roof of the car in a parking lot that night. That's that thug shit. That's that I don't give a fuck shit. It's crazy, but in a way you like it. I'm like a bag of Jolly Ranchers.

You never know what you're going to get. You just have to be ready and on point. Just stay ready and don't ever get caught slippin'. You have to be able to match my randomness. Show me that you are kinky and wild. That's how you can keep me interested. Your physical appearance also has to be on point, but that's vice versa as well. I respect the game if you feel the same. I'm not sensitive. I can take it.

Ok, ladies, let's get into some other shit. You have to realize that things you did with your last dude don't always work with the next dude. So, don't set yourself up with putting your sex and pussy on a pedestal because when you do that you open yourself up for failure. Many women think they know the correct way of doing things, but it's always more than one way to do something and that goes both ways. So, let's talk about how I like getting head. You've got to become one with the dick.

You have to build a relationship with it. You have to care for the dick and love it. You also have to act like it's alive; like it has its own feelings, and it's not a part of my body. Caress and stroke it as if it's a baby pup. You have to be gentle. I should feel like you care more for the D than me. Matter of fact you got to cuff that dick as if it's food and you don't want nobody digging in your plate. Have foreplay and gently place kisses on him. Give him smooches and give him tongue kisses. Sing into the microphone. You gotta hum on that dick; practice your vocals. Make sure your mouth is moist and wet as if you were sucking on a lollipop. You know them nice, hard, and juicy blow pops. And that's just starting off with the head of the monster.

Next, you gone make the D transform into a Popsicle. This is when some of your skill comes in. It's almost like you're dancing and trying to see how low you can go. Now, you're not trying to throw up on the dick just go as low as you can take it. Make sure you keep your mouth nice and wet on the dick while you sucking. Make sure in the midst of you sucking you come back up to the head because the head is the most sensitive part. While you're sucking and bobbing on that dick, make sure you got a hand gripped on that dick so that you can stoke while you're sucking. Not just any type of stroke. You want to swish your hand in a circular motion. Not rough but with a little firmness in it. The only way that you can be doing this right is if you are really enjoying it. You're probably moaning more than he is and your vagina should be getting real wet. That's when you know it's real.

Now you're not done yet. You have to continue going. One thing that you have to understand is just as much you want your box ate, as long as you want it, a man wants that too. Now you can start treating it like a blunt that you are about to roll. You know lick it sideways, up and down, and make sure that you are making eye contact. Don't be afraid to look up and show him that you are enjoying it. When you look up, I'll probably be looking down at you, mouth wide open and head tilted back, especially if you're doing it right. As soon as you see that his eyes are closed or as soon as you notice that he's in a trance, cuff the nuts and massage as you go. Make sure you're sucking and massaging real good. That part is going to drive him crazy. If you're really nasty, suck on them balls.

Keep doing those things. Just mix up the orders. Depending on how you're feeling, you can do it until I nut, or you can do it until I'm hard enough then hop on it. You better do it before I do. If you do decide to do it until I nut, that's where you have to determine how freaky you are going to be. Either you're going to let me do it in your mouth or you can decide where I can put it at. It depends on how nasty you want to be. Let's talk about the other part. You know that deep penetration shit. Since we're talking about you, we're not going to talk about what I'm going to do in a bedroom. We're going to talk about your performance. Let's talk about that horseback riding shit. That drop zone roller coaster shit. If you want to show me how you get down, treat me like a woman—throw me and flip me and fuck me everywhere.

Now, I don't know about throwing my legs up to the moon. I ain't down with that. You have to ease me into some shit like that. Just know my ass is off-limits. I don't play that. You can start out laying me back on the bed and putting the condom on me. I don't know if we like that or not. Just hop up on there and straddle to where you can put your hands on my chest. In order to do this position or even start, you got to make sure your nails did. I'm the roughneck type. I am on that thug-loving heavy. Gone dig them pretty ass nails in my chest or arms. Don't get carried away, little mama. I ain't trying to bleed. I really hate that shit, but I like that shit during sex. Damn, I think I just gave you permission to scratch me up, huh. I don't know. I might have to rethink that.

Ride that muthafucking dick. Don't be scared of it. Go on and make them ugly ass faces you be making while trying to be all cute and shit. You know wiggle that ass down on that dick. Don't be afraid of heights. Twirl them hips and move that ass in a circle. Shit, I'm like a female. Take your time up there. Don't be going crazy. You ain't in no race. Yeah, I know you like how that feels, don't you? I see you up there with one hand on my stomach. My fault, just keep your motions. After you ride that thing and you're looking into my eyes kissing me. I want you to get your heavy ass up. I want to see that ass get in that reverse cowgirl for me, Mami. Grab my legs so you can hold on and lean forward. I should be able to see Barbados. You know everything —you know that water, that moon, and of course me standing in the middle of the ocean.

After you do that for a little while, get up, and force me to another part of the house. Something like the kitchen. Sit me down on the chair. Get on the top, ride, and face me, that way I can lift both of your legs and take control by lifting you up and down and pounding you at the same time watching your titties jump and seeing your hair stick to your face from the sweat build up. I want my lap to be soaking wet. I want us to moan in each other's ears and then we can take it to the couch. I want to see that pretty ass arch in your back.

I want to see that upside-down arch that your ass makes when it's upside down. That when I slide up in you make sure you keep that arch in your back because I know it likes to disappear once that D is in you. So, you know we're really going to get into it. Shit, you fuck around and we'll take this shit to the patio, straight up, not giving a damn. If somebody walks past us, they just walk past. You can do so much to keep it exciting. THAT'S HOW YOU MAKE LOVE TO A THUG! We're going to talk about another form of thug loving in the next chapter. There is a lot to fall under thug loving than what we just spoke on. Yes, ladies, no more sex talking for y'all freaks. Shit, I might write a whole book on that after this.

Chapter Fifteen

Ride or Die

Thug Love

Thug love is a passionate yet challenging love. It's that Bonnie and Clyde type of loving. We accept each other, yet my love is much stronger than regular love, because I know we are going to ride for each other. She knows who I am and where I am from. That's all that matters. I can be who I am because she welcomes it. Maybe it's because she's really fascinated by it. I make her want to learn more. She wants to be a student. Hell, it's starting to rub off on her. I may be able to control her, but she catches herself doing the same things that she sees me do naturally. You're slowly becoming a thug misses. You're developing some of the features and traits of a thug, but in different ways.

Thug misses: a female that is thuggish, but is still ladylike and drowns herself in knowledge about the street and where she's from. (SD)

You may not be into what I am into as far as actually doing some of the dangerous stuff, but you got what it takes. You done studied so much 'til you can do whatever if it comes down to it. You are now the number one person that I trust, only because I showed you the ropes, and I know whose side you're on. If you didn't come under me, then I couldn't trust you. I mean, you're loyal to who gives you the game, but you still carry that cutthroat, by any means mythology. Don't be surprised if you tell yourself that you want to be a part of the action because sometimes it's already in you to do it.

Sometimes it's not, but it develops once you're around someone like me. I said it's in you because you know a lot of women come up in households that are so strict, mainly because you're a girl. You felt or feel imprisoned. The problem is that parents are so strict and give you only an inch of freedom until you actually want to be loud. Sometimes being so strict can cause a good girl gone bad because she feels cooped up and buried while everybody is having fun. You feel left out of life and start feeling like you have a lot of catching up to do. Especially hearing everyone talk about how exciting it really is. So, when you are with someone like me, it's different. You know you will get in trouble if you talk to me, and that alone excites you. So now, you feel you are down with catching up on the phone.

Many times, the thrill of being caught turns people on. It's adventurous and exciting. It's a roller coaster, and you can't wait to try it out. Many women do it because they feel it's almost mandatory or it's an obligation to do so. Meaning get down or be a thug, and a lot just wants to do it. Others have already been embedded with it like me. Mama was in the streets doing what had to be done to handle bills and so on. Daddy was always out on the corners doing what he was doing, and her brother was skipping school, robbing, and hustling. It ran through her family, so she was destined to be something anyway.

Ride or Die: a girl or woman who sticks by her partner through thick and thin. Even at times when it's dangerous to herself, a ride or die, a woman, is loyal at all costs. (17)

Yes, thug misses and ride or die chicks have their similarities, but this stage is when the ship done crossed over in your deep end. This means I'm here forever and in deep whatever happens, happens. You're in the game like AE. There's no turning back. Now you're actually learning a lot. You went from studying and learning me to learning the game. I got to build you up with no fear and confidence in whatever you're doing. You got to know what the consequences are for your actions. You always have to know the worst that could happen because if not you'll break down when it does come. Knowing this will help you choose which way to go because you'll understand what comes with it and decide if you can handle it. You will always have to watch the streets. Its goal is to swallow you whole like a freak that enjoys giving you head.

If you hit the level of ride or die, that means that you are willing to be on some Tasha and Ghost type love. So, whatever happens, I got you and am with you. Type of shit on some I don't want to die, but if I have to I will type of love. Some if you shoot, I shoot, if you fight I fight, if you rob I rob type of love and so on. Believe it or not some of y'all chicks be acting like y'all are ready, but y'all ain't ready fa real. Would you fold if the police got you or threatened you with time? You ain't Cookie off Empire. You can't do 17 years and come back without being for self, or maybe you can. I mean, it's not like that all the time, but if it is then ask yourself if you gone ride. Can you be loyal? Can you keep your heart in your chest when shit hits the fan?

A thug misses is loyal and can be trusted. She's more of the one that can accept what I do. She may do small non-major stuff, but that's about it. I love either one of them. Fa real as long as I can trust her, and she's loyal, then I'm with it. You got to be careful because either you can be way deep or in too deep. Sometimes there is no escape zone. It depends on the caliber of the thug that you are. Like I said, I'm more mixed, but we'll get into that later because I know you want to know what that means.

Chapter Sixteen

Breed With A Hustler

As I told you before, I am bred with a hustler. So yeah, it's time to talk that hustling shit.

Hustling: doing whatever you got to do to get that bag, having the ambition and drive to get money. (SD)

Yes, these two topics have several similarities, but they also have their differences. They just do things a certain way, and they are not really into the spotlight. Hustlers are not really into the things that the thugs be on. I guess that I can still say that because I'm a representative of the hustlers too. Let's just dive into the lifestyle and what is on this side of the bloodline. I am so focused on that bag that it is crazy. I think it's all that I see sometimes. Like sometimes, women flock to me, or sometimes I don't see them until they're all in my face and my personal space. It's different for all hustlers, though. You got a bunch of different types of hustlers. So, you gotta watch out for the one you choose, and you also have to realize that their motives are different. Here are the names of just a few.

Gym Shoe Hustler: They just do it for the new Jordan's and LeBron's that cost $250 or greater. They buy them and then cop an outfit to match. Then when they go to the club, they have no money for drinks or food because they spent all on their fit. (SD)

Trick Hustlers: These dudes hustle just to trick it off with some random females to have sex. We call it trickin'. (SD)

Nickel and Dime Hustlers: These are the ones out here putting their freedom at risk for $100. They're not trying to really secure that bag but are putting on a front like they really are. (SD)

In The Way Hustlers: These are similar to the nickel and dime hustlers. They are just in the way and out here trying to sell a bunch of bullshit. The little stuff they are selling ain't worth it at all. They're not trying to grow or hustle for themselves to survive but to keep on messing up their money because they know somebody will front them a pack, which is also another word for drugs. (SD)

Drug Dealers: These are the ones that are getting to that money or trying to get that money. They are really trying to get rich. Sometimes you can tell by their attire and the things they have. They are most likely coppin' from their own plugs or connects striving to build an empire. Needing to know when to quit is their only obstacle. (SD)

The list goes on. I'm more of a selling drugs type, but I'll do what I got to do to get that bag other than sell my soul. Messing with my type, I love to have a ride or die female with me. A female that loves to get that bag, because when I'm doing what I do I know that my rider will keep the others in line when it's time to move. Shit, most of the time she's down to get her hands dirty as well. She's the one that I trust the most to get whatever needs to be done, done.

So, with that being said, are you really down for my type, are you scared, do you think that you need to be a stay at home woman? You don't have to see nothing, but you will know that I'm out here trying to make a way. So yes, ladies you may scream get a job, but realize everybody can't get a job. A regular job doesn't always take care of all the responsibilities. For instance, say I have a woman with a child or with more than one child and all of the bills that come with that. Working at a fast food restaurant or retail store isn't enough fa real. It's just slaving for pennies when I can make more than the law and everybody else. In six months, I can have a couple of thousand dollars.

The world got to respect a person's hustle. Not all are good, but it is what it is. People have to do whatever they are good at. Some are good at stripping while some are good at drug dealing, boosting, and robbing, etc. Not everybody can be lawyers, dentists, bankers, and so on. Nobody's perfect, but bills and things have to be taken care of. Who are we to judge? Instead of judging, how about giving out some jobs or whatever. Ladies this isn't directed at you, but it's part of the lifestyle that I'm in, so it needs to be said.

I said I am not into the spotlight, but it still finds its way to me even when I move lite. It's mostly because people can't stay hushed. Everybody just sit, talk, and gossip. Not saying the spotlight means talking to the police. I mean just spreading around rumors that I am getting money. Now that can lead to police interaction because the wrong person could catch wind, and they could be working with the police or may get in trouble and bring me up. That's why I try to keep a low profile. I realized I'd do better staying clean and not getting my hands dirty by all means. I must say I still like to enjoy the fruits of my labor, though. I come from a life of struggle and pain.

Single parent mothers are working like hell to make sure the bills are paid. I come from having to take food stamps and buy something so we can get cash back to take care of things at home. I come from depending on churches to give us donations and Salvation Armies to provide us with food bags and hygiene products. There's no telling what others have gone through and how they've lived. However, most likely, we all want to or have wanted to live a better life. So, yes, I most definitely wanted to get everything I've always wanted fa real, fa real.

I started with getting my appearance up and keeping it up when I do. It's a blessing coming from three to four outfits to having almost an outfit for every day of the month. I went from one pair of shoes to match everything when it didn't in the past. So now, my closet is looking like Finish Line. I went from a soup bowl haircut to a Caesar with a nice beard. I mean from going from riding an old school Cruiser with a mongoose bike to riding in an old school Cutlass with 24-inch rims. My trunk's got stupid speakers with TVs all in it. I worked hard for it, and I grew up wanting it; able to live comfortably, not wanting for nothing, and being able to do what I want when I want. So when I get there, and I hustle, I hustle hard like Ace Hood.

It's not a game to me, so when I see these dudes out here faking or fleecing (selling fake dope) people, I be ready to move. I don't need people messing up the money because when they mess up the money, it's a problem. When that happens, the thug side of me really emerges, and it's bad intentions from there. I'm not a gangsta, but I can come as one if need be. So, ladies, it can be a rocky road at times, but you just gotta keep riding.

With every good situation or all the living it up that we are doing, it's always the flip side of things. In this game, it's really almost impossible to trust people around you. Nowadays, your own family will turn against you for that old mighty dollar. Some families will turn against you for a female even faster than money. I worry about a lot of things when I'm out there. I'm going to list a few.

- Jealous / Jealousy

- Fear

- Broke People

- Jack Boys

- Police

- Disloyalty, Gossiping, and Hate

These six things are some of the things to look for and worry about when you're hustling. All of these things have two things in common, which is life or death. There is just so much hate in the world and you have to you hide from it. Everywhere you turn, it's there whether it's from family or friends or the streets period.

Jealous: to feel or show envy of someone for their achievements and advantages (18)

Jealousy: the state or feeling of being jealous (19)

There is always somebody that is jealous of me and wants what I have or want to be where I am or at least better than me. They really want to be me and in my shoes. Jealousy can stem from more than just the money. It can come from what I got, to the woman that I have, or how all the women that flock to me. It eats at them to the point they pray for my downfall or demise. Instead of just going and getting their own, they plot on how to get mine. They're not   jackboys or dope boys. They feel like they should be where I am driving my car, spending my money, or even sexing my girl. Shit, sometimes it may get so mentally crazy for them that they think my kid's should be theirs.

There are no limits to what they will do to get what they want. Whether it's them setting me up so that my woman can leave me, whether they've sent someone to try to take what I possess, or whether they send the police knocking at my door so that they can arrest me. When I say my door I mean put the police on to what I'm doing. They may pay someone to take out the picture period. If need be, they might be obsessed with being me. This person can be family friends or maybe someone who doesn't even know who I am on a personal level. It could be someone just watching or someone who's heard who I am and what I do. They've heard so many stories they damn near feel like they've been knowing me forever. Now, I'm walking around unaware there is someone jealous as all outdoors of me knowing how I move, and now they're secretly plotting on me.

Fear: an unpleasant emotion caused by the belief that someone or

something is dangerous, likely to cause pain or a threat. (20)

When it comes to me as a hustler, people can fear me, but then again, they may not. However, since I'm no ordinary hustle, there is fear. Why? Don't forget I am a thug before anything. So, if you don't remember what that is, let me remind you. So yeah, there can be fear, but it all depends on how serious I am taking my hustle. Things can get very cold if need be or if I feel people need to be put in line. If you play with my money, or if you try some foul play type games, things can get real. The next will sound crazy and contradicting, but it can get real if I catch you stealing from me. I say that because I never stole from a person, plus robbing, and stealing are different. I'd rather you rob me like a G then take from me.

Fear can be introduced when it gets to the point when people try me and I let it go because it wasn't too serious. But then it starts to get out of hand to where I got to put the press out on you. For example, I give you some drugs to sell, you later mess up some money, and this is your second or third time. Three strikes and you're out, well really two. Now I gotta put hands on 'em. I got to let 'em know it's not a game. People in the hood try you and think it's a game 'cause you haven't put in work, so now you gotta start making examples outta people. It could be putting hands on them. I could be letting my goons do it or even worse may have to result in gunplay. What they are not gonna do is play with me like it's cool. You gotta feel my wrath. Now you've awakened a monsta, a whole other side of me that just emerged.

Now people start to fear me and be paranoid of what I am capable of. The streets have turned me into a terror. I become a straight gangsta 'cause somebody playing with me and mine. I'm on some get them before they think about plotting on me, and once I do once, it's like I might as well do it again if I got to. Now not only am I becoming a gangsta, but I also gain power when I apply pressure. I'm now feared because I make dudes do dirty work for me, so it becomes easier to apply fear.

A Broke Person: one who has little to nothing. This person is either broke as hell or has chump change. (SD)

In my opinion, a broke person is a desperate person. They are always in need of something or some money. These types of people are just as dangerous and have similarities to a thug, a hustler, and someone jealous but are not quite either. A broke person, like a thug, will do whatever they gotta do to make something happen when broke. They will steal and boast if they get the opportunity and turn around and sell it to me or whoever else is interested in what they have. Just that fast, they turned into a hustler, because if they choose to steal over little side jobs around the hood or whatever, they're hustling, and that's their hustle.

At the same time, they may be jealous at times where they see things and want it, or see people and wanna be them. Now their mind gets brainwashed and has them asking themselves, "What makes him so damn special?" A lot can trigger anger and jealousy in people. Sometimes by picking on 'em about being bum can cause jealousy every time you're around. They start to become easy to brainwash. Now, people can talk them into setting me up and in return, they'll get some money out the deal. They become threats, or they get persuaded to possibly cause harm. If they hear the right amount, being offered to them, they'll at least think about it if anything.

Jackboy: a thief; a person who commits robberies mainly into robbing hustlers and big-time drug dealers. (SD)

With similarities to a thug, these dudes are on another level. They rob people for a living. It's their hustle. It's what they have become very good at. They were most likely thugs. Hell, most start from thugs, so I guess we're all mixed breeds. Jackboys are very bold though. They'll be in the hood like everybody doesn't know who they are. Most jackboys don't rob dealers in the hood because we all most likely went to school together or know each other from doing silly things growing up. Now they will get the ones that are scary as hell or the people they don't like from other hoods, of course. Most of the time, it goes like this for newcomers, other cities and states unless they are newcomers themselves. Then everybody's up for being targeted.

They are the ones that don't really be out because they don't know us, and we don't know them. They probably move to our area from their area, or they know and mess with a female from our side. These dudes will rob you for whatever you have on you at the time. They'll rob you and demand everything you got period. They'll go as far as taking you home to rob you too. They'll kidnap you or your family and hold them for ransom. They'll do whatever to get what I got. Sometimes they'll just keep robbing every time they get a chance to, but sometimes it's the way it's done that makes it even scarier and dangerous for it to be life or death.

It is important whether they wear a mask or not; if they wear a mask, there's a good chance you'll be ok if you comply. If there's no mask, either they know you're scared and will do nothing, they plan on taking your life after they get what they want, or they just plain don't care. It's like yea I did that. Wait…they could just be stupid as hell and armatures. You can never trust these dudes, and I mean never. I don't care how cool y'all are.

Police: the civil force of national or local government responsible for

the prevention and detention of crime and the maintenance

of public order. (21)

I think everybody knows why they are dangerous to someone in my profession. Even outside of my profession they are harmful to society; some of them. Like the others, they are jealous, haters, hustlers, and they're even jackboys. They are thugs. They do whatever to get that check also. Some are about keeping the streets safe, but some are corrupt and crooked as a question mark.

If you look at history, police have always had it out for my type. There has always been hate for us. I don't know if it's because we make so much money, and it's so much that it makes their money look like spending money. It could be because their families are on drugs, wish they could have the stuff we can afford, or the beautiful women we come across. It may be because their woman or daughter has been fascinated with street dudes. Plus, once you go black you never go back. Everybody wants to experience that thug loving at least one time or have at least thought about it. Some women hate my color so maybe not those, haha.

The cops take lives every day. There's no real hustlers these days, but still, you can't put it past them at all. They will still kick in the door and take everything they can and arrest you. Sometimes they won't arrest you. Sometimes they just rob you of what you got. However, they're jackboys if they arrest you for a big bust, and they only turn in a certain amount while pocketing the rest. You're probably asking why they don't arrest you sometimes, right? Because they may find nothing on you but money, and they know where the money comes from, but there's no proof. Therefore, they just take your money and leave you be because they're crooked. They may not if it's something that can't get you put away for a long time, so they take it, and step on it in front of you. Some may arrest you just to do it, knowing I'll be out in 30 minutes tops.

I must say when they do have it out for you they'll do whatever to get you caught up. They'll plant drugs or weapons and all. If they start running out of patience, the crooked ones will. They just wanna bury it not by death, but by life in prison or close. This is still life or death. Then there's the crooked ones I gotta pay to not take me down, but shit, that's the games. It's kinda like a level of chess for me.

Gossiping: exaggeration or fabrication of a story regarding somebody other than the person telling the story. Talking about someone when they're not around. Slandering or tarnishing this person's reputation. (SD)

These people have nothing to do but talk and gossip about everybody else but themselves. Once they get word of anything you already know everyone is gonna know, and that makes them dangerous because they aren't into the streets, so there were no rules. Therefore, it was like you had to make sure they knew nothing. They are also a danger because all a person has to do is take some beer to their house, drink, sit back, listen, and ask questions.

Depending on who it was, it could be some nosey ass gossiping ass female's gossiping. You could get any info from them if you play your cards right. Now you have the ups on the enemy, and if they want somebody they could probably get them. If the police needed info, they would find out because people talk too damn much. At this point, the info done hit the wrong hands, and it could be life or death. People got to stop talking about everybody's business and worry about theirs.

Disloyalty: a broken vow or promise. A breach of allegiance to turn on a team player for the other side. (SD)

This one can have a little bit of all in it. In fact, it's made up of all the things I previously named and more. So many things can actually occur to make a person become disloyal. A person sometimes becomes disloyal if they feel they are not treated how they feel they should be treated. These types of people are more dangerous because they are actually part of your circle. Therefore, they are more dangerous than the rest because they actually know the ends and outs of the system

I'm running. They probably know a lot of personal shit, depending on how close we were, such as where I live and my family. Which is why I don't let too many get close. If this is one of them I am definitely in a lot of trouble.

I don't treat my people bad. Some do, but in a lot of cases, they want your spot just like the jealous ones, and when they don't get it, their mind starts thinking about going to other places. It's like basketball. You've been loyal to a team, but you wanna be let's say number one like Kyrie, but you got someone who's better like LeBron. It doesn't matter how many rings you win. You still want your own team or to be number one. So now, you ask to be traded. "No shade, Kyrie. I love, bro. He's the raw PG I've ever seen." Now he becomes a threat in different ways because he threatens to get knee surgery if he's not traded; that's a threat.

If you got someone on your team that doesn't wanna be there, they could do whatever to sabotage the team's second threat. If you do trade him, and he's not the enemy, he still knows the whole system so now it can be used against you. Lastly, now you gotta face him, and he was your number two before, but now he's number one. If he was your gunner you have a problem cause he's the worst enemy you can ever have. It's like your fighting yourself, and you know every combination of combos you're gonna throw so you can counter all.

This person can also be one that is disloyal by just communicating or talking to an enemy of yours. They don't believe in, if I don't mess with 'em, you're not supposed to. I can't trust you because I don't know who your loyalty is to. If I don't mess wit 'em, and you do, I can't trust you because I don't know who your loyalty is to. Shit, for all I know, you're setting me up for a downfall. There's really no winning because there's always someone like this in your circle. What extent is their disloyalty? This is the big question.

Hate: feels intense or passionate dislike for (someone) (22)

In the Bible, this word means murder or wishing it upon someone. (23) I don't know if I really have to write much on this one. I think that this is very self-explanatory. They all have its identity, but are all a form of each other. These things are life or death situations. So, I gotta be careful who I trust and who I let get close to me. That's why ladies it's good to know some of my background so that you can see why I don't trust like that and see why I am the way I am.

Chapter Seventeen
Street & Book Smarts

With street smarts, you should have a few skills that'll help you survive in the hood. Mainly because it's easy to get led astray.

- Blending In

- Common Sense

- Outsmarting

- Seeing Through People

- Communication

Blending in is one of those important things because if you can blend in, you can see a lot and get in as deep as you choose. You're like a human chameleon. You can become or adapt to any setting. With this, you can gain a lot of trust and friends that are into whatever it is you're trying to blend with. It's not easy to blend in. Sometimes it can take years and years of work and dedication. Sometimes you gotta show that you're worthy or you are what you want to be. Know you don't just step to the top of the ladder. You gotta climb up one step at a time. You gotta get along with people knowing what to ask and not to ask while never over crossing the boundaries but also be assertive.

Assertive: speaking and behaving confidently but also direct

so that people pay attention to you. (SD)

So for women, you gotta almost be a man. You must have his way and move how he moves when you're out in the streets. Know what you're doing and never let off fear. You're in the middle of a gang of wolves so you can be a sheep, or you can be a wolf, which one would you be? Blend in, and don't be afraid because remember you're with me and I gotcha back all the way. If you're gonna be a hustler, study, and become a hustler. If you're gonna be a gangsta, become it. Know that you can do everything that comes with it. You gotta be like Kobe

Bryant and study the game. Study those that resemble what you are or are trying to become. Become great but be greater because it's already bad enough that they don't take women seriously or as an actual threat. When they count you out, make 'em count you in.

The bad thing about common sense is that it can't really be taught, but then again, it can be. Honestly, there's too much that can't be taught. I think common sense is something that parents are supposed to teach their kids; when it comes to the streets, that's on me. At the same time, you gotta have the ability to learn. If you have a learning disability, then yea, it can't be taught. You gotta know who to trust and who to be around, or you'll get swallowed up and spit out. And not having common sense is a huge flaw. It's dangerous not only to yourself but for me because whatever you do falls back on me. If you can't see normal things that just don't make sense, that's a problem. You should be able to see what doesn't.

If you're in a hood that ain't yours and you see people clutching their guns when they see you. Common sense should tell you that you shouldn't be there. It should tell you something ain't right and that something crazy is probably about to happen. Or let's say you get into with a female, and she comes to wherever you're at with three other girls. And she says, "I want a one on one and you by yourself." That should tell you you're gonna get jumped if you do. You just gotta use your head to stop being naïve and blind to reality. It's not a game.

Learn to outsmart the enemy. The game is like chess. You gotta know your move and next move before the opposition. Not only know your moves, but also know their moves as well. You have to set it up to where the things you do only give them a certain amount of moves and certain moves in general. Don't leave them with endless moves because now you've set yourself up to be beaten, and that's not the object of the game. All these things need to be learned if you want to be with me. Yea, I am creating a monsta, but that's what you asked for. Don't go taking this knowledge and doing the opposite, like running the streets. This for the thug misses to the thug.

The easiest way to outsmart people is being both street and book smart. People are being both street and book smart cause now you have so many tactics to create and to destroy. A lot of street dudes are just mainly street smart. They didn't try going to school. They dropped out or never went. They think they are naturally both, but that ain't how it works. You have some that are tough and might still even be in school while they thuggin'. You have some that are straight dumb. They like learning as they go or attempt to, but no one takes 'em serious. So, of course, having both puts you on a higher level. You're valuable to the streets, well to me you are. You'll think of smarter ways to do things and come up. Hopefully, get out the game to make legal and secure money.

Being able to see through people is a good gift to have also. If you can't see through people, they could use that as a weapon that could prosper for them. This goes back to where I talked about all the different things that could be life or death. All of those things will be able to attack and take over your empire and leave you for dead; that can be literal. So observe and study those around you.

If you can see through a person that's also like chess, cause now, it's like seeing their move before they make them. You'll be able to see the fake ones that claim they got your back, but they don't and who are steady talking about you behind your back when you're not around. Being able to see who's loyal to you is important because people tend to act as if they know the game, or they act like they can see through people. Still, it can be opposite sides. Like that person who says they are really for you. You'll feel that they're a fraud. The ones that really ain't, you'll see them as the ones for you. Why in life do you think you realize many people, including yourself, had fake friends? They snitched, stole from you, set you up, sexed your partner and so on. It's due to people not being able to see through people sometimes.

You just gotta be careful who we call our friends and associates. Shit, even family falls in here because if it came down to it, they'd do you bad too. Remember that. Family tends to be the first to stab you in the back anyway. Family knows how to get in your head better than the regular person. They'll try and do everything in their power to make you see that I'm a no-good ass street dude that's gonna end up dead or in jail like the folks said all black men would be. It's bad because they'll try setting up ways to get you to turn on me. They would go to any extent. They'll start treating you like you're a baby or like you're a young, dumb, naïve little girl. They'll try to make decisions for you and lecture you as if you can't think for yourself. Your family will have you thinking I got you hostage or under a spell. Even worse scared or something since you're with me and telling them you're not leaving me. You just gotta be able to see through everything, even myself. It's good to be able to see through me. And it's good for your decision-making on how you wanna move with me.

Having good communication is very important because like the law says everything you say can be used against you. You got to choose your words wisely when you're in these streets. People hold you accountable and things can be life or death. When arguing with people, know your opponent. Know how far things can go and ask if you can handle whatever comes with it, or is it worth it at the end of the day. Especially when we're tryna secure the bag. As I said before, whatever you do falls back on me.

You also have to speak with confidence. Know your shit. Any sign of hesitation or unsureness, and they'll be on you like flies on shit. Bad communication skills can kill relationships in the streets and can cause crazy atmospheres. You gotta have great customer service, and most importantly, be respectful. You gotta respect the game. It's the only way to play. Being street smart and book smart makes things even better 'cause now you can break shit down like a shotgun. It'll be as if you've been doing this since birth, or you're the Griselda Blanco of the game.

You gotta know when someone is speaking to you in code and when they're communicating to others in code. It's survival tactics. There's a lot of Spanglish (street talk). You gotta use instincts. Sometimes it could save your life. There's so much to learn when you're dealing with me. I live a fast life, so it's a lot of fast learning, sometimes on the go, to be done. Therefore, you gotta ask yourself, do you want to be out here with me, do you wanna just let me do what I do, sit back, gain knowledge, get education, and become something even more important to me.

This money gotta be accounted for. Do I need you here to do that anyway? I don't want you to feel you gotta be in these streets. You don't have to prove you can be out here. Prove you can finish school and get a degree or something. However, if you do decide to be out here, I'm not knocking your decision at all cause you'll still play a huge part in this

empire.

If you learn different types of languages, you would also be on another level because now we have the upper hand on knowing things and getting to new levels of the game. Please know with any career that you want to pursue and anything that you want to be, I promise to support. I need you to be great. In fact, I'd rather you have a career then to be out here. The enemy tends to think when we're doing so much street business with our girl, a part of it that they see it as a weakness. They see it that way because they know you're now a part of the rules of the game.

They'll see you as a target depending on how deep you are, or we are. You gotta be willing to take it to any level if your hand is tested. If you're low profile and out the way, it's less likely they pay any attention. You could do either and still be low profile. Be like Slim, the baby brother from Cash Money. He's like a ghost to everything. You rarely even see him. Any real hustler will support and back you on reaching career goals. You just gotta be serious and go get it with no hesitation and no fall offs.

Chapter Eighteen

Stack That Money

The game is different from having a job or career. With a job, you can look for a check every week or bi-weekly, and that money is accounted for. That money goes to bills and what you spend it on. Your money is your money. No one can take it from you. That's what we call Legal money.

Legal money: money accounted for, honest money that gets

state and federal taxes taken from it. (SD)

You have no worries when you're getting that legal money. Well, the only concern is making enough to take care of yourself and what responsibilities you may have. With legal money, you have to be satisfied with your income. You have to be strong-minded to struggle and not fall into hustlin'. In fact, let's not make hustle seem like it's always bad. It's not always bad because there are two ways two hustle. Can you tell me what those two ways are? Yes, legal or illegal are your two ways. A lot may say there are a thousand ways to hustle, but no, there are two. There are a thousand things to do regardless of each option. So, you can have a job and still hustle the legal way.

If you're a woman, you can do things such as doing hair on the side, babysitting, house cleaning, catering to old people, or by cooking, and selling food. On the flip side, fellas can do things such as wash clothes, cut grass, fix cars, fix things around the house, and bounce as a security guard at a club. All of those things are hustles. Some people hear the word hustle and automatically think negative. To me, it is just thinking one-dimensionally fa real. Whatever you're doing outside of a 9 to 5 is a side hustle. You out there grindin'. When you make legal money you can buy cars, houses, jewelry, and own businesses without getting caught up as long as you're handling your business correctly. Now that I think about it. You can get caught if you're not paying taxes and so on. Nevertheless, if you're doing everything by the book, you can't lose unless your business does badly. If people don't have a demand for what you're doing, then you have to change it up.

There's nothing like being able to do whatever you want when you want and how you want without worry about the law. You get pulled over, and you're okay because you have everything correct and legal. So, what if you got $5,000 in the car and it's yours? It's accounted for and everything is good. It's beautiful to have checks coming on payday. If you're making enough to where you can splurge, you know no matter what you get, more checks are coming behind that one. So you don't gotta worry about feeling overwhelmed about too many responsibilities. Therefore, the money looks even better. You can survive and live off that check you're making and still get those Gucci's and red bottoms that you always wanted.

Hell, some people are born into the family business. They just get a job and house and so on. Some haven't felt the struggle or had to live in the belly of the beast. Therefore, they don't know what it's like to be hungry, cold, trying to keep warm with no lights or heat with the baby at an early age nor a family looking down on you. Many times, it's their fault because they brought you into a world of struggle when you couldn't fend for yourself. They look at you because you're struggling, and it eats at them. They may feel you're a disgrace when you're really mirror of them, and they made that path for you. Now, you're tired and want to get off your ass and get a bag. There is nothing wrong with that. Yeah, those people were fortunate not to have to go through it. The ones that have are much stronger because they learn how to eat from the fruits of the land. So, if anything happens on earth like The Walking Dead shit, we'll survive, and they'll look to us to show them how to survive.

Illegal money: not taxed, not accounted for, dirty money. In other words, dishonest money. There are two different types of this money. (SD)

Dirty money: profit from the sale of drugs, prostitution, guns, or other illegal activities. Money that needs to be laundered. (SD)

Blood money: money acquired through killing. A fee paid to a hired killer or money that came from the taking of someone's life that ended up in your hands to be passed on throughout life. (SD)

This money is what it is. The police hate it because they know how much can be made when someone is illegally hustling. I can sell heroin for six months and not have to work another day or hustle again in my life. What officers, prosecutors, and judges make in a year, I can make in a month. They see us living our best lives in a few months while they've been working for eight years and still have to for another thirty years just to retire and collect 401K. Their 401K is just chump change to us. Just look at the statistics of a hustler in the streets-them being deceased or killed:

• Pablo Escobar - $30 billion

- Griselda Blanco - $2 billion

- Freeway Ricky - $600 million

- ElChapo - $14 billion

Now let's compare that to the salary to police officers. The average salary of a police patrol officer is between $52K to $62K a year. Do you see now why they hate hustlers? LOL. It's because they only make chump change when hustlers become millionaires. However, that's why most are crooked, because they need more money. One of the reasons why the law hates drugs is because it can't be taxed. Why do you think they are starting to legalize marijuana? They are smartening up. Through their work experience they believe that 90% of the world is smoking weed every day. So they like, let's just legalize it and make some money so now they become drug dealers. LOL. In my eyes, they are now hustlers. If you can't beat them, join them, I guess.

Illegal money, of course, has its negatives. Well, it's always going to be negative to people. However, you can't move how you want or would like to because you don't want that attention from the law. So, you got $5,000 on you, but this time it's dirty money. When they stop you, if you can't show proof or check stubs saying how you got it, they can confiscate it. After this happens, they'll give you a certain amount of days to show proof and to claim it. If you can't show proof and you don't go and get it, guess what, they keep your money. I know this from experience.

I can say the law loves hustlers because it's free money. If they stop you and they already know you sell dope or drugs, they know that they can confiscate your money. A lot will take it and pocket it for themselves. Anything you purchase they will investigate, especially a business. That's why people launder money, push it using other people's names to keep the heat off them and get the money cleaned up.

I know you're asking what does this have to do with you. Well, you got a secure that bag when you're out here in these streets. Remember, when you're illegal, you got to keep money for a lawyer too. You need getaway, bond, and canteen money. You got to have some away just in case that day comes, or just in case they come seize everything. You can't be spending like you can do a nine-to-five check. They can come and take all your money and all your assets at any moment, and there's nothing you can do about it if it's not accounted for. They know it is from illegal activities. I'm not saying don't enjoy life, but stack for those things you don't want. Trust me, to get caught slippin' is not a good look.

Get that money, but figure out what you can do to make it clean. That's why I need you to be book and street smart. Check into investing, overseas accounts and stocks. You do not want to be in this for life. It's never a good ending. We get greedy when we count up hundreds of thousands of dollars, and want more and more.

The first we say is "This the last time" and end up being more times. Then it's a few more months, "We're done" then it becomes years. Especially, when you're running through money like hell. First, you'll want to get a Benz. Then after you get it, you'll want a Benz truck, and after that you'll want a lot of jewelry and so on. I mean, that's cool, but you gotta keep that to a minimum. Be smart, cuz again, we got to think about the unwanted attention we'll be drawing once we start balling out.

This is the knowledge you have to know, not just me, you feel me? That's why I say just stay fine as hell and let me boss up for us. I need you to smart up for us because with all the money that we're about to make, I'mma need you to clean it up, fa real fa real. I know you want to be the baddest, at least I hope you do, which we're going to talk about next since we are on that topic. Just think about what could happen if I was to get locked up or even worse killed. If you've depended on me, you're in trouble now; we're in trouble. Always stack for just in case, which will also be talked about more later.

This money gotta be accounted for. I need you to do that anyway. I don't want you to feel you gotta be in the streets. You don't have to prove you can be out here. Show you can finish school and get a degree or something. However, if you do decide to be out here, I'm not knocking your decision at all because you'll still play a huge part in this empire.

Chapter Nineteen

Stay On Fleek

It's highly recommended that you stay on top of your game when it comes to me. I expect you to represent me just as much as I represent you. Whether you are street or not, that doesn't mean you get a pass to look ratchet. I'm accepting nothing less than a dime piece. Matter of fact, you got to be a dollar piece. Just because you're with me doesn't mean you're not still in competition to keep me. Shit, nine times out of ten when we met, you were on fleek. It had better not stop. You've got to keep that same energy. There's no more letting up and no falling back. Apply that pressure, even more, if anything. You've been upgraded not downgraded, so there's no excuse not to still be the baddest woman walking.

When I see you, I want to feel myself get excited. I want to bite my lips, grab my -ish and act as if I've never had you. If I don't give you that demeanor, bae, you're falling off, fa real fa real. Do you think Beyoncé walks around looking tore up when she's with Jay? Hell no, she going to look like him like a billion dollars, no if, and, or buts about it. Have you seen one time where Michelle Obama came halfway representing Barack? You're a queen. You've got to be royalty to his loyalty. If you're always ready, you never have to get ready. You never know what may transpire. You ever seen Tasha come half-steppin' with Ghost on Power? Nah, she was ready and Queen like. Whether they had differences or not, she was always on top of her game.

When I use my eyes to look at you, I want my day to get better. I want to be proud and feel lucky to have you. At the same time, don't let it get to your head and make you start feeling yourself to the point where you start acting attitudish or new. A lot of women start seeing all their beauty merge and start feeling like I'mma zero, and they are the ones that stand by me and make me a dime. Stay in your zone, live right, and be grateful. Don't start thinking you need nothing or no one.

I mean, like how Nick Cannon did on *Love Don't Cost a Thing*. He forgot where he came from. He got on top of his game with her help, and he tried to appear too good for her. He started acting like he was just hot shit, and she was nothing once he saw how fly he could get and how everybody started giving him attention.

Always remember trust and loyalty goes further than looks and what money can buy. It can only get you but so far. When you hit a wall and can't go for it any more your only choice is to go back in the direction you just came from to get to where you are now. Ladies, I have to realize looks are only really seen as sex, so you start getting over yourself because you are feeling like the shit. You lose somebody like me only to realize now you got to have a bunch of sex to get what you want and get things done. When you were over here, I gave you the keys to get what you wanted and needed. You looked good and all that without paying with sex. That's why it's good to secure that bag and to live a life like this and not have to do things that you don't want to do.

Please note the only reason that we did sex during these times was that you were mine, and I was yours, not cause you needed stuff. There is a difference. So be careful and know what things mean in-depth to outsiders. The devil's name was Lucifer. He was the prince of music when he was in Heaven. He was living his best life he could until he wanted to be God or better. He started to feel himself too much and so much that he got thrown out of Heaven and dropped here on Earth. Forever a castaway with no way of going back. (Isaiah 14:12-16)

You just gotta play your part and let the King be King. Live your best life cause you can easily get dropped and thrown out of the empire. Now, you're watching somebody take your spot and become happy as all outdoors. While listening to Shys Debiocci's song "Suppose Ta Be Us" looking crazy, wishing you hadn't acted up and hoped that you could make things right so you can be as happy as you know that new chick is going to be.

Staying on top of yourself should be a given anyway. Things like that should be in your nature. Things I did say I should not even have to spend a lot of time on because you are made to be beautiful. So, just be that. Yes, you're going to have your days, and that's cool because I will too, but bounce back and get it together. That's how you stay on top of your game and be a queen. I'mma always have your back. Hell, it's probably my money taking care of everything, so that's even more of a must if you do not have to pay for stuff for yourself all the time.

In the last chapter, I talked about stacking your money up. So yes, that's your money, but things like self-appearance can still be done. When I say stack I mean, try not to start buying too many cars and very expensive things. That doesn't include getting your hair, nails, feet, and all that other stuff done. I like seeing them pretty ass hands and nails around my dick. Sometimes I feel like those nails sliding across my back and holdin' the back of my head. Get those feet done because I'm not into feeling no hard ass brick mason feet rubbing across my legs at night, or feeling some ate up looking toes and nails scratching me up.

Your feet better not stink either. Go get that Vicky secret you supposed to have plenty of that it's nothing like seeing them panties creased up and all that booty. Lord, I don't want to see no mismatch panties and bra unless it's color-coordinated with the outfit you're wearing. Your crazy ass probably thinking,"Well I don't wear panties anyway." Y'all stay letting it air out, I guess. Y'all better put something over your vagina before mosquitos fly out there and take a bite of that that peach, or even worse, some fruit flies get up there. If they get a taste of that peach they going to harass you like I do, except they just going to eat on you freely whenever they like.

Get your wardrobe up as well. You got to be able to have a variety of things to put on, but you got to know what to put on. It got to be nice. I'm not saying that got to be designer all the time, because we know a woman can shop at Wal-mart and Payless and still be one of the baddest walking. I mean just put your stuff together with respect for what you are; just that the baddest thing walking. I can't lie. I see you in some red bottoms, some Gucci, and I know you would destroy that shit to. If that's what you desire, work hard for it. Get that bag so there's nothing you can't cop. That's why I want you to know how to get to the bag as well. You can have your own bag and you won't need to ask for anything. You can go get it whenever you want.

Chapter Twenty

Jail

This is one of the lowest parts of being in the streets. The lowest times in my life were when I went from providing to needing to be provided for. There's so much to talk about in this chapter, but it's real stuff that will be addressed. First things first, this is why it's good to stack that money because this can happen when dealing with dirty or bloody money. This is why I teach you the game and let you know what's what because going to jail is another just in case times in life.

You got to know how to handle being with a man like me. I can't just let you live life with no experience in the streets. If I had just let you be, then we would be in bad shape because you're left trying to figure out what in the hell you're gonna do to pay for this and that. I taught you the ins and outs hopefully if this day came, you would be

A-1 with it. If so, you already know where the money is and what to do with it. You already know to hit the lawyer up and pay him to come get me or to be ready period. You know to start moving shit, start closing and relocating shit. I don't gotta call and explain nothing because you're with it. You're a boss. You know its loyalty and trust. So whatever happens, it's a locked bond that can't be broken.

Are you ready for things as such? Are you prepared for the police to start kicking in doors with guns drawn and raiding? Are you ready for an interrogation hearing, a bunch of lies, and he says she says, and bad cop good cop things? Can you keep your stomach calm when they say 20-30 years, but just be trying to scare the shit out you? You should be equipped to be able to go flip the money we got saved up. Do not take this time to go living your best life. You gotta stick to stacking that money. It's about to get a lot harder for you because now everything you are taught is about to be tested.

Are you going to stand up and boss up? Or will you fold up like paper and let us crash? I am not saying don't wait. Of course, let the heat die down before anything, especially to see what the deal with me is. However, if it looks like I got to sit tight for a while, you got to make a decision. If you didn't learn anything as far as the streets, use your book smart to flip and clean any money that hasn't been cleaned. Figure out what you can do to make the money multiply. You still have to still be able to live, be good, and hold me down while I am away. Don't let yourself go underwater because once it's gone it's gone It's like starting from zero. Then there would become times of desperation because everything will start to tumble down. Any burden would fall on your shoulders. Burden is defined as something that holds you down— usually a worry or a sore point that you don't share with his close friends or family. (SD)

Then you start to feel like a burden when you start to talk to people about your problems. The man that gave you the game and helped you live well becomes a bother. He's calling, asking why didn't you send canteen, asking why the phone's off going to voicemail, and why haven't you come to see him. You're too ashamed to tell him you messed up the money being irresponsible and making dumb decisions. The first thing I will think is you messed up the money and you out there trying to get back right.

However, as time passed, I will think like all the other dudes in here. You done ran off with somebody else and living good off the hard work that I labored; stacked money for a better living for us. Especially if I got some years to do. You figure "Oh well that's a long time, and there's no need in waiting." I have to say at that point you left me for dead. You said fuck it and broke the bond of trust and loyalty. Yes, any man would be pissed, but I would thank the hustle god for showing me who you really were all this time.

When I say hustlers, I mean my hustlers that are no longer here that watch over us fellow hustlers. I don't say God because I know God doesn't probably approve of what I've done or doing to profit in life. To me, it's like who's to say it's wrong to play the game of life like I am. This is really a game of survival and advancing trying to get around the board until the game is done. I'll save that for another book, though. I just had to shed some light on that meaning.

I would respect you much more as a woman if you kept me up-to-date on your troubles. Tell me you got a plan to tighten up your mistakes.

Or tell me "Hey, guess I messed up the money babe. I did start messing with somebody. He's temporary, though. I'm just going to use him and his resources to bounce back and stack again." Even if you tried some X, but it didn't fall through, and you took an L, I won't be mad. I respect the game. Get money to survive. I guess he's the one dishing out the money you're sending, huh. Shit, I still see the lock on trust and loyalty. Just keep me on point. I'll play along and show you where to go to get shit back poppin' now. I'll play my position. I'll be good on no letters, visits, or calls as much because I understand.

The problem comes when you do none of this and just disappear off the face of the earth. It's not even a problem. I just know now what I got to do to carry on until I get out of here. It's crunch time. I have to make what I can out of a dead and lonesome highway. There's no need to get deep in my feelings because you played a foul ball. I got to hit home runs now and bounce back. I got the mind and smarts to run a whole operation behind these walls.

We all know you got a million different types of dudes that are in prison. Not all are the same thing. The only thing you can say is they are all criminals. Truthfully, not everyone there is bad. You have some that are wrongfully convicted. You got those that are there for conspiracy just having knowledge of a crime. Some are just drug users and regular old minor things, and so on. I say this because I will show you a difference and comparison between one of those dudes and me. I know that many people are not going to like this, well those types of dudes, and I know some women who actually need this knowledge. This book is for y'all, so I'm going to keep it real since you want to know what y'all have to do and why we are the way we are.

Let's start with a regular ole thug. He might be in for having a few grams of crack and maybe a warrant he had for probation violation. Now, he got to lie down for ten years because he pled out to it; he had a public defender. He didn't really have too much of anything other than maybe a few hundred or a stack or two put up. He owned a Crown Vic with some rusted rims on it with a crazy sound system and a TV upfront. He lives with you in your section 8 apartment in the projects. His name is not on it because you're not supposed to have a felon staying there. He got two or three kids under eight years old, but

Maybe or maybe not with you.

He only hustles like two or three grams and swears he's out there getting to that money at the same time knowing he has a warrant. He says to himself he's just going to run if they tried to stop him. He sells to anybody coming through there. He knows some and some he's never seen before. He got a gun in the trashcan near where he's trappin' by the bodega. The gun is rusted and keeps jamming when he tries to shoot it on days they shoot fireworks. He has six golds up top and four at the bottom of his mouth that he never takes out to clean, and they are just pullouts. He's also fucking two or three ratchets females.

He's locked up, and now he's left you with the couple hundred he had left from copping those same grams he got caught up with. He keeps calling you to send some money, not giving two damns that the money ran out; which you didn't even spend any of it because you're loyal to him for some reason. I can do nothing but salute that trust and loyalty.

You're doing all you can to work and take care of that little girl he left with you to raise alone for at least eight of the ten years he played. Every time he called while in the county before sentencing and knowing his plea, he cursed you out for some dumb shit, embarrassing you at a visit to show off in front of a bunch of dudes that really feel some type of way that he doing you like that. You're starting to slowly fall back from him.

The lawyer told you it ain't really looking good for him, not to mention he's going in front of a judge that lost his mom to a bad batch of crack. You're trying to be strong and ignore the verbal abuse because he's mad all the money he saved is gone because you're giving it to some nigga you're supposedly sexing. When again, in reality, it was only $560, and he ran out by going through that in the six months that he has been in the county. He tells you how slack you are, that you are a whore, and he's done with you. He claims he'll be out soon and that his case is petty.

You began to fall off and only come through every once in a while because he is still your daughter's father. You're not looking to be with anybody. You just know you got to focus on making sure y'all are good without him. He's been sentenced. Now he's realizing that none of them girls he was smashing dealing with him fa real fa real. He starts to think about you and what not and tells himself he's got to get back in good with you because you were and always was all he had.

Now you're talkin' to him. He feels more concerned and interested in how you've been. At this time, he's been shipped to prison. It's been six months since he was in court and got ten years. He's asking about your moms, the family, and your work life. He says things to see if you got a man yet like "I know your man's happy for you." Your response is "I don't have one of those. I don't got time. I got to worry about me and this little one of yours." Once that's said, he's going to start trying to reclaim his throne or his spot. The goal is to start making you smile and laugh again.

He's got to make you wanna tell him more; which will bring more money sent for phone calls. Then there will be a lot more "Bae" or "Babes" instead of your name. Then those visits will start increasing because he's going to tell you he wants to see you and his daughter more. He wants to make up for lost time. He misses y'all a lot, and he's working on his ways and wanna do better. He'll start telling y'all he wants to be with you, and he thinks he wants to marry you and be a family. He's sorry for the things he took you through. He needs you to please forgive him, tells you that he's been going to church, and so on. Then you'll start receiving jailhouse cards, holiday cards, and creative shit as such. Things that'll make you say, "Aww." Your heart will be open again as it was when you first started talking to him.

He's going to learn so much slick stuff to tell you that comes from all the other men he's there with. Ultimately, you fall in love with the words of other men that he's using to win you over again. He needs you to ride his bid out with him because everybody else died off from riding with his bullshit. He got you thinking that he's a different person, and everything is going to be okay. You gotta ask yourself is what he is saying real or in the moment.

I'm different. I'm not going through all that. It's either I'mma be with you and if not I'll tell you. Don't get it twisted. I may do some of the things. Let's say similar. Things like making sure you enjoy our conversations and visits. However, I'm going to be too busy trying to hustle and send money home like hustling to the point where people are going to be getting with you, with my new for me. Dude could be keeping it real, but I think he's feeding you whatever he has to so that he can make his bid easier. He knows once he gets out he probably will pay you no mind. You will be old news. He'll be hot shit. I can't knock him. He's doing what he's supposed to do. He's making plays. You got to go by your own knowledge and see if he's real. As I said before, it is hard, but it's a risk you gotta ask yourself if you want to take.

I'm not throwing shade, but it's lame as hell because he's being selfish to his child if he's leading you on just to do you bad once he's out. That's where we are even more different because I'm going to be like take care of my daughter. Don't worry about no canteen. I'll be okay. I left y'all out there struggling because I was nickel-and-diming. Ladies, you can tell how he was before he got locked up. If he's worth the risk, accept whatever it is you get and live with it but don't complain later.

Now, me in the situation, after I got played, yes, like I said, I will find a hustle, and I'll get me a pen pal, but I refuse to feed them a bunch of lies. I'm going to be real about all off top and be sure they know I just need a friend and whatever happens happens. If I do begin showing love or my feelings it'll only be real emotions. This will be because she's talkin' that bag talk, has career plans, wants to help replace my last, and actually do what she was supposed to do. She's probably going to stack or flip money I give her, and money I have people send her from people in here. Their people on the street are gonna be forwarding her money for me.

Because, again, I'm getting my own money. I would have figured out a hustle, and she has gained a little trust out of me to do so. She actually makes some power moves. Yeah, I got to give her some thug loving, some real loving though, no play-play. When I tell you I'm marrying you when I come home, I will. You held me down. If you keep that trust and loyalty for life, it's 'til death do us part. You got to show me that even through the toughest times you're there to stay, that you are suited and booted to climb over or go through any obstacle. I want to feel, with confidence, no matter what happened that I could depend on you to be here when I look over. I want to know that you could hold it down and go to put in work to make sure I'm good coming home. When Gucci Mane went to jail his last time for five years, Keyshia held him down. She didn't just leave him hanging.

Keyshia Ka'Oir flipped the money he left her. He left her two million dollars. She took that money and flipped it into businesses. She adapted herself to healthy eating like he was to adapt to his eating. She started working on their dream home and had six million waiting on him when he came home. She made sure he stayed eating healthy, worked out with him, kept him off drugs, and out the streets. She kept it going. She wasn't for herself. She held him down; that's loyalty at its finest. And guess what he did?

He proposed to her with a 25-carat ring and married her. That's that stuff that'll get you proposed to and on lockdown. Yeah, I'll be quick to run as soon as a man gets locked up or takes a loss, leave him for dead type of female who has no loyalty shows up at my door. Now, yes, there's some you got to leave for dead because maybe they deserve it, but don't do it to the ones that have been there for you and yours. You know he'll bounce back at any given moment. Stop feeling like you're so much better without him when you're not. Stop thinking about taking the easier route. I want you to ride and get dirty with me. Show me it's real. Just as you want to hear baby it's going to be alright. I want to hear it as well. I'm not like the others. I don't believe in selling dreams.

Selling dreams: To feed someone a bunch of lies. Giving
them the imagination to see a story that's perfect with
a white picket fence. (SD)

These things are often called promises. Promises that will most likely be broken. I don't sell you a story because I don't know what's to come as far as natural life. I can tell you what I want to do and accomplish. I wouldn't lie to someone I call my ride or die. That kills the trust. I'd not tell you certain things though, if it's better you not get into it. Others will tell you whatever they got to tell you to make you become a puppet.

People say I am breaking code speaking on all of this, but if you don't know, you'll be easily persuaded to turn on someone that's 1000 with you. People would be able to use you to be the Black Widow and destroy your lover, and once that happens, you go from a Queen to a pawn on the chessboard. Only now, you're stuck on the other side, never being able to go back to your best life.

Most men want you to be dumb to the things he does and smart at to all other things. They don't realize how valuable you are. You're an asset. The queen can move the same way the other pieces do, except the horse. That means if you move right and think about future moves, you will take no L's. That Queen is going to do everything it takes to protect and cater to the King. So even if I go to jail or prison, remember you're still supposed to do what you do, but go even harder.

Chapter Twenty-One

Never Pressure Me

Ladies, I know how y'all roll. I know most women do not want to be alone. You do not want to sleep alone or go out alone. You just do not want to be alone. Y'all even call up somebody you can sex to go to events with you because you want to go with someone. You really don't want people even knowing you're alone. You tell me to come with you, and that is just a little event. You're not going to tell people I'm your man, so I don't need to worry. She will say your guy friend instead, which another way of saying this is who I am with sexually. So, I don't really trip. I mean, cause for one, you're probably bad as hell anyway, but we haven't gotten to the stage of relationship status like together.

It's a work in progress right now. I'm focused on this bag, and depending on where we are or how long we've been talkin'. We probably just friends and free to do whatever we please. Which means you could be dealing with someone else, and I could be dealing with someone else as well. You never know. We do have that understanding, though. What we got going on is what we got going on. It's just we probably have been talkin' and sexin' and a whole lot more, but it's still what it is. We're single and just messing around.

Ladies, I believe y'all be down for whatever when you meet a guy, and y'all say y'all aren't looking for a relationship right now either, or that you're trying to get yourself together, and you just came out of the relationship also. You just want a friend like I do, but is that really the case? Do you and can you just want a friend? Can you truly handle just being friends? I don't really know if that's truly even possible, well possible only in other situations. I'll talk about it later. Maybe your intentions are good at first, but then it disappears. I don't know.

What do you think will happen when we talk, and you're

constantly smiling and laughing your heart out all the time? You're going to love talkin' to me and grow to want that conversation more and more, which is completely normal, but that may be where I make my mistake. Maybe I should have kept my conversations to a minimum and not have them often. But how would I do that if we're friends? What kind of friendship should be established between us? Like are we fuck friends? Are we best friends? Are we friends with conversation? Are we Facebook friends? Are we Instagram friends? Are we Twitter friends? Snapchat? What are we?

I guess it's friends with benefits and that we need convo or some sex. We're always there for each other. Or maybe we're that until we find a person to be in a relationship with. Maybe you don't want to have sex with a bunch of people as a woman, so you'd rather have someone you can do those things with instead of having multiple partners. Nevertheless, can you really accept just being friends? You claim you're okay with it, but is that ready the case? It keeps coming back to that question.

What's going to happen when you start chilling and doing fun things with me? You're going to want to do more and more fun things because you enjoy yourself a whole lot when you're with me. I am leading you on by saying shit like we can go catch a movie or get some food. In the very beginning, because it's nothing to it, and we both know it. We just chill like two people building a friendship and not trying to be bored on boring days. So can I really take you out when I feel like it is just boring? Or cuz I want a woman's company? Hell, we may decide to go out and do things on a regular, not no romantic shit, just simply fun shit. How would you carry yourself in public? Are you going to try holding hands? Are you going to want to try to be all over me? Are you going to want to put on a body language to show and make it seem as if we're together?

I think 80% of women that go out with someone they are friends with the long way (also sex partners) will find themselves getting attached to the man. Sometimes you may not even realize you're doing it. If I said something to her about it, I believe you would be shocked that you were acting in such a way since we are just friends. I must say, with the shoe on the other foot, 80% of men would also act that way, especially if you are a dime piece to him. I think the only time neither would act that out is if y'all out and there are other dudes peeping, she won't really do all that, "I'm with him" gestures because, at those moments, they remember they are single and can do whatever.

You may not go talking to another man or let one talk to you because of respect. However, it'll be directly known that you're not with me and vice versa with the man. He'll be the same way though, fa real fa real. So, now I can't place it all on women because men will do it to you. You will even see an early stage of jealousy. It won't be too deep, but you'll see it and feel it; I promise. Only you will notice it, though, and again he or she won't even believe you or realize it at that point that they are acting like they are. They'll deny it to the end. They will never admit they felt some type of way about that situation.

What's going to happen when we start having sex? That's one of the big ones that have to be answered. When physical contact takes place I know I am about to touch feelings and emotions within deep down. I think it's going to be really hard, almost impossible to just still remain friends, especially when I put all this D on you. That thug love and starts the drip all over your heart and soul. I can hear you saying now you're still going to be good, that you don't let the D control you, or make you do things you don't want to do. You're going to say everything that sounds good to persuade yourself that you're good and too strong. You're going to say what you think I want to hear, or what I want to hear. Because I told you I just want a friend and you agree to ride with that. However, as time passes, sex is kicking in, and you are happy. Hoping that we will be a couple. Nothing would make you happier because you're accustomed to all that fun and sex.

At this point, you're afraid to speak on how you are feeling, and you might even tell yourself "I love this man." You dare not say it aloud cuz you know you're going to scare me off. You understand you're tripping, so you tried to straighten up, and you tell yourself let me fall back for a day or two. You're trying to break out of that trance. You want to shake it off and stick to the rules, but it's hard. The plan is to make it so you can seal the feelings and act as if nothing is wrong. You've convinced yourself that you never strayed away from the agreement, knowing deep inside that you did and almost got lost along the way.

Your emotions start to get on your back like in a visible pile of weights you can't remove. Things start to get confusing, and you begin to lose your thoughts of the things that we agreed on from the beginning. Family and friends start to be in your ears telling you "He ain't shit" when, in all actuality, they don't even know me personally. They probably didn't or haven't even had a conversation with me and feel they can say things are such about me. Why do they say it? They think I am playing you, because we're not in a relationship yet. But you're always talking about me, or they have never met me face-to-face, so they feel I'm not good enough for you or good to you.

It's so crazy how people try to live your life or determine your happiness for you. They tell you that you can do better and stop selling it for him cuz he wants to be single. They tell you that you need to leave me alone and stop wasting your time. They probably think I'm just some thug you messing with, even though they are actually correct. I am a thug, but it's different over here. Maybe you can do better. Perhaps you're wasting your time. Only you can decide; not them. Seeing they don't know what we got going on. It's not anybody's business, but they don't have to make me out to be a bad guy.

Can you just be friends, or will you breach the contract? It's a question you got to ask yourself when you're alone and thinking for real. Do you fall back and look for true love and a man that you could try to claim to be yours? Are you going to risk going to see if the grass is greener on the other side? Do you ride it out until the wheels fall off? Do you keep the happiness you do have until maybe that one comes and finds you? Or perhaps you and I do end up together. You never know life throws curve balls.

When everyone is in your ears, and your heart starts to attack your mind, you begin to develop reactions. These reactions become pressure, and it is like being with your back against the wall. Now you've been brainwashed to question what I want from you and how do I feel about you. Questions that should not be asked because it's not a question that can be asked on the level we're on. It's an uncomfortable question, knowing what you and I agree to live by, and the friendship we share.

You got to be careful with the things you say and ask. You got to be careful with what you do as well because it all can make the situation awkward from then on. It'll make me feel like I need to fall back and keep it at a low level, meaning cut convos down to maybe a few times a week and cut out going out because it's too much. We'll definitely have to cut down on sex because things could really get out of hand.

No man wants to feel pressure to do or say anything he is not ready to say. Like you tell me, you miss me and in the same breath ask me if I missed you. Like just cuz you missed me doesn't mean I missed you. Women force and pressure men to answer you by saying things like, "Damn I said I missed you or I said I love you," and being mad when I don't respond or say it back. I tell you I don't miss you, or I don't feel the same, and you get in your feelings and start to act differently. You try to pressure me to lie so that you can feel good about telling me how you feel. You have too much pride to say how you felt without me having to say it back.

If you miss me, okay, fine, say you miss me. I feel you. Thanks for letting me know. If I missed you, I told you or said back to you. I see you two times a week, we talk every day on the phone and so on. So why do I feel I have to miss you? There's no need to because it isn't like it's been weeks. It's only been two hours since the last time we talked and saw each other. That's not enough time for me to miss you. You should not pressure a man to do anything because you feel you're ready, so he should be too. You're ready to be in a friendship? Okay, but that doesn't mean I am. You're ready to be married. Okay, I hear you. You're this, and you're that, right? You believe you're prepared for all of those things until it doesn't go the way you planned.

Imagine you pressure a guy to be in a relationship with you, or you pressure him into getting married, and he was not ready. He doesn't even know why he agreed. He realizes he's in something that he doesn't want to be a part of. Now the relationship gets sour, and now you're wide open to getting hurt at any moment. Now, you're crying and going crazy because you felt he supposed to love you, and he's a cheater and a no-good nigga. You are asking him why he married you and broke your heart, and embarrass you as he did. It's because you forced it. You press them into being with you by telling your fam and friends you think I'm going to propose to you one day, that you know I will always keep you happy, and so on.

Since you made me feel obligated to have to be with you, I didn't even want to be with you at all in that way. You're going to be even saltier than ever hearing me say I was forcing this. I didn't want to be with you in that way. Do not pressure or make a man feel obligated. It will be in turn out to be no good. You got to let him move when he's comfortable or vice versa. It will feel amazing to you when I start sharing those particular words.

Obligation: doing something you may not like or even enjoy doing. What you do out of respect or some profound sense of duty. (SD)

Pressure: the continuous physical force exerted on or against an object by something in contact with it. The use of persuasion, influence, or intimidation to make someone do something. (24)

Chapter Twenty-Two

Cold Emotions

I don't possess hard feelings or emotions. I'm not into the whole sensitive thing. I've always said that was a weakness and a flaw when you're thuggin' for real. It's kryptonite to a man. It's already bad you carry traits and genes that can make a man almost be your slave or puppet. A thug in his feelings is not good. It leaves me wide open to be caught off guard in the streets. That's one of my biggest fears. Real talk, I don't ever want to be in my feelings over nobody but family. You're probably asking yourself how do I love or show it then. You can love and not be caught up deeply to the point where you find yourself tripping about someone. Like when I say I don't want to be in my feelings, I mean, I don't want to be on no jealous kick. I don't want to be trying to figure out where you're going or who you're talkin' to and texting.

I don't want to be sensitive at all. Let's get that straight. That is for females. I feel any man that is emotional or gets emotional for a woman needs something else; most likely some help. I feel if I'm in my emotions, and so are you, who is the lion in the relationship? Men got to leave that sensitive and emotional stuff to y'all women and be a man. Even though emotions are not always bad, I still feel it's not for my breed of a man, so don't expect me to be with all that lovey-dovey type thing. No, I'm not with that.

I'm so street that I don't even like for you to be too sensitive, and then you're feeling so deep. Saying babe a thousand times gets annoying for real. I don't like it too much. I think that sometimes you get too emotional, and it starts to sound like a child. That's being sickening because they want something. Like, don't mess with me knowing I'm a G. I'm not with it. Then getting in your feelings cuz I don't be doing all that cuddling shit. Don't start that baby why you don't ever call me crap when you know when you met me I wasn't really calling you or hitting you up.

Sometimes it may take time for me to loosen up and start texting more but, don't pressure me. As we start to spend more time six months later or so, I'll hit you every now and again or text you more. I'm trying to get that bag, so I need to be focused. Plus, it seems like all you want to do is be on the phone quiet for 12 hours; that's not for me. That's time wasted and pointless. Don't expect what you got from Jonathan from me because he was a good dude and wasn't into or raised how I was. We are two different people. Don't tell me all the things he did involving feelings and emotions cause I don't care. Take this thug love and respect it like you did when we first met. That's a start.

Again, do not pressure me to do or say certain stuff. You tell me. What he did or what you are what you look for to try obligating me to do those things. I bust pipes. You can't bust me, so stop with the change-up all of a sudden. And if your feelings and emotions start to shift and you want to be done or leave, remember I don't give a damn. My care for you can be turned off within seconds. It doesn't matter how long we've been talkin'. You'll put in your mind so fast and tell yourself I'll never care for you.

I stick to what I do, and I let life run its course, so if I start to soften up for you, so be it. Whatever happens, I let it run. I'm just not into the sensitive stuff. Respect that, and we can go far. I would do some nice things and treat you to some good stuff. I may take you and spoil you and put something special together for you if I'm in the mood and feeling you a lot. So, I'm not saying I'm just a robot. I'm just saying let me share the way I feel comfortable. It's more genuine than when you do allow me to be me. You got to be patient. When you rush, you run into a wall of failure.

I know we spoke about a woman's feelings before, but it's just so much that it branches from them that it has to be spoken on again. It's just very dangerous, so I think most of the time it's in a man's best interest to keep it at a limit. However, it is confusing because how do we know if there's a limit. I feel sometimes I can touch a woman, and she'll be like we're together now or even deeper just by my touch. This is why I'm the way that I am with being brutally honest. It makes it hard for you to want more from me.

It takes a different kind to deal with the true street dude. It's not just glitz and glamour. You have the bad times that can make you feel like you're in too deep, and you realize maybe you're cut out for it. Maybe just maybe you stick with being cool and not trying to fall deep. It's crazy cuz some of you women are so crazy that I can talk the most shit and hurt every little feeling you have, and you will stick around or fall even more for me. It's weird. It's not true because it just takes a second to think about all the verbal and emotional abuse you've endured over the years ordering relationships. Then think about how much you've forgiven and continued on in the relationship. It's a woman's feelings and emotions.

It's good, but at the same time, it's bad cause constant forgiveness and accepting can evolve into evil. It's not healthy at all, and I'm not talking about the point of you forgiving, but for the stages of emotions that your mind puts you through. I think a lot of the time, it's our fault because some people just lead on the emotion and sell your heart false dreams. Your hopes get high only to be driven full speed into the prevent.

Feelings: an emotional state or reaction. The emotional side of

someone's character and emotional responses or

tendencies to respond. (25)

Emotions: a natural instinct and state of mind deriving from one's

circumstances, mood, or relationships with others. (26)

To me I feel, emotions are event-driven, while feelings are learned behaviors that are usually cocooned or hidden until awakened by an external event that changes everything. Primitive emotions emerge from deep within but not from the cerebral, which is linked with the thinking and also the planning in people. Feelings tell us how to live. Emotions tell us what we "like" and "dislike. Feelings state there is a right and wrong way to be. Emotions indicate there are good and bad actions. Feelings state your emotions matter. They express that the external world matters.

Feelings establish our long-term attitude toward reality. Emotions determine our initial attitude toward reality. Feelings alert us to anticipated dangers and prepare us for action. Emotions alert us to immediate dangers and prepare us for battle. Feelings ensure the long-term survival of self (body and mind). Emotions ensure the immediate survival of self (body and mind). Feelings are low-key but sustainable. Emotions are intense but temporary. Happiness is a feeling. Joy is an emotion.

Worry is a feeling. Fear is an emotion. Contentment is a feeling. Enthusiasm is an emotion. Bitterness is a feeling. Anger is an emotion. Love is a feeling. Attraction is an emotion. Emotions can be measured objectively by blood flow, brain activity, facial expressions, and body stance. Emotions are carried out by the limbic system, our emotional processing center.

Limbic system: a complex system of nerves and networks in the brain. It involves several areas near the edge of the cortex concerned with instinct and mood. It controls the basic emotions (fear, pleasure, anger) and drives (hunger, sex, dominance, care of offspring). (27)

Yes, I have no emotions. Some people may say I'm a sociopath, but in the real world, they're basically the same thing. I think you are looking for the word alexithymia. Alexithymia lacks "the inability to recognize or describe one's own emotions." (28) Just because someone is Alexithymia doesn't mean they lack a conscience. I read somewhere, not sure where, that it is thought that around 10% of the population suffers from the condition. In some cases, it's almost twice as high in males.

Alexithymia is characterized by a difficulty identifying feelings or distinguishing between them, a difficulty describing feelings to others, a limited constructive imagination and an inability to express fantasies (a difficulty with creative imagination). (29) Alexithymics can only feel anything via external stimulus or externally oriented. There are two types of Alexithymia, primary and secondary. Primary is a long-lasting psychological condition that never changes. Secondary is temporarily caused by a stressful situation that fades once the situation changes. (30) No, I am not or close to a sociopath or a psychopath we know what they look like and in to. That's not me though they feel it has its comparisons it's not who I am.

Sociopath: a person with a personality disorder manifesting itself in extreme antisocial attitudes and behavior and a lack of conscience. (31)

Psychopath: a person suffering from a chronic mental disorder with abnormal or violent social behavior. (32)

Like the sociopath, I do not have a personality disorder. Yes, I have multiple personalities, but I think everybody does. If they say they don't, they're lying because everybody's got another side. The word used for that is not sociopath. It's alter ego.

Alter Ego: a person's secondary or alternative personality. (33)

An alter ego is a second self, which is believed to be distinct from a person's normal or true original personality. Here are a few examples of alter egos with famous superheroes.

- Bruce Wayne's alter ego is Batman
- Clark Kent's alter ego is Superman
- David Banner's alter ego is the Hulk
- Barack Obama's alter ego is the 44th president.
- Peter Parker alter ego is Spider-Man.

Do you think they were all sociopaths? No, they weren't. There's a big difference to me. I'll give you some examples of some well-known sociopaths you may know. An article from healthyplace.com entitled "Most Famous Sociopaths To Ever Walk The Earth" discuss well known sociopaths.

"John Gacy lived in Des Plaines, Illinois. He was the epitome of both local and national citizenship, receiving a Man of the Year award from his city's Junior Chamber of Commerce and separately taking his picture with Rosalynn Carter, the First Lady at the time. He entertained kids as a clown at their birthday parties. People adored him. What they didn't know, because he hid it so skillfully, was that he also happened to be a sociopath. One of the most famous sociopaths to ever walk the earth. In the 1970s, he murdered 33 young men and buried most of them in the crawl space under his house."

"Ted Bundy was an attractive, charismatic young man living in Seattle in the 1970s. He lured women to him with his charm. Dozens fell prey and were brutally beaten and murdered by his hands. He was so well-liked that he got away with it for quite some time."

"Jeffrey MacDonald had power and admiration as an officer in the Green Berets, a medical doctor, and family man. He was a husband, the father of two daughters with another child on the way, and he was a narcissistic sociopath who brutally murdered his pregnant wife and daughters."

"Jeffrey Dahmer, the Milwaukee Cannibal, raped, murdered, dismembered, and sometimes ate 17 boys and men in the 70s and 80s."

Famous Sociopaths But Not Serial Killers

"Jack Henry Abbott was a respected and highly praised author when the crime of forgery sent him to prison. He actually didn't commit murder until he was in prison where he stabbed someone. Upon escaping from prison, he robbed a bank, and was sent back. He contacted famous author Norman Mailer (who was not in prison but was in the world writing novels, plays, films, and the like) and convinced Mailer to help him write a book. Out of prison, he charmed his way into Mailer's literary circle in New York and enjoyed attention for a few weeks. When a waiter wouldn't let him use the employee bathroom in a restaurant, Abbott stabbed him to death and returned to prison. He died by suicide in prison in 2002, but his sociopath charm lives on."

"Joey Buttafuoco has never committed murder, but he gained fame nonetheless. His affair with teenage, Amy Fisher and Fisher's attempted murder of his then-wife, Mary Jo, thrust him into the spotlight. His charismatic behavior captivated the media and gained him national attention, further fueling what Mary Jo termed his sociopathic tendencies. While he isn't a murderer, Mary Jo says Joey Buttafuoco is a sociopath, albeit a famous sociopath."

Well Known Female Sociopaths

There are less female sociopaths than male. Males "commit more violent crimes and to be the famous sociopath serial killers. Still, female sociopaths are famous criminals, too." "Diane Downs was after a man who didn't want children. To get what she wanted, (him) so she murdered her children." "Deidre Hunt played an equal role with Constantine Paspalakis in torturing and murdering a young man. They videotaped the whole thing, presumably for their own pleasure and entertainment."

So if you try to compare me to a psychopath, you're the one with a mental problem for real for real. I'm nowhere near either facts. But again I will show you examples of psychopaths and what they like and create from and collect human remains, since you don't know.

- Nine masks of human skin

- Bowls made from human skulls

- Ten female heads with the tops sawed off

- Human skin covering several chair seats

- Head in a paper bag

- Head in a burlap sack

- Nine vulvas in a shoe box

- Skulls on his bedposts

- Organs in the refrigerator

- A pair of lips on a draw string for a window shade

- A belt made from human female nipples

- A lampshade made from the skin from a human face.

- According to murderpedia.com has biographies about many serial killers including the following.

Edward Gein

Edward Gein was a notorious serial killer and grave robber. He is the inspiration for famous horror movie villains such as Norman Bates and Leatherface. There is not much more to say about Ed Gein. He was a psychopath that was obsessed with his mother until her death in 1945. After which he started exhuming the bodies of recently buried women, on which he performed acts of necrophilia. He also chopped off pieces of their bodies and used them as trophies. He then graduated to murder and murdered two victims before being caught by the police. He was written off as criminally insane and eventually died in a mental health institution.

Dennis Rader

Dennis Rader, (also known as the "BTK Killer" which stands for Bind, Torture, and Kill) was a serial killer who murdered 10 people in Kansas from 1974 through 1991. He was known for taunting the media and the police with letters describing the murders he had committed. He would bind, torture, and then kill his victims as his name suggests.

Reportedly, he strangled his victims until they lost consciousness, waited until they came to, and repeated the process, forcing them to experience near-death until he would finally kill them, and ejaculate on their bodies. He was eventually caught when the police discovered metadata in a floppy disk he had sent to them, which inadvertently contained his name and his place of work. He is currently serving 10 consecutive life sentences.

Charles Manson

Charles Manson was the leader of a cult known as the "Manson Family," which he started after relocating to San Francisco, following his release from prison. Many of the murders were not actually carried out by Manson himself, but by his "family". He was a self-professed Scientologist who brainwashed his followers (mainly female) into believing an apocalyptic message was embedded in the song "Helter Skelter" by the Beatles. He was convinced that a racial war between whites and blacks was impending, and that the blacks would win if the family did not intervene. He also believed that the entire Beatles album on which Helter Skelter had been recorded was specifically meant for them. Charles Manson was convicted of the crimes committed by his "Family" and is currently serving out a life sentence.

Nannie "Giggling Granny" Doss

When you hear the phrase "Giggling Granny," you probably think about someone's cute grandma—not a raging psycho killer who nearly wiped out her entire family. Nannie Doss, native of Blue Mountain, Alabama, was a seemingly normal and happy neighbor and wife. They keyword here is seemingly. Over the span of about 30 years, Mrs. Doss managed to kill at least ten family members, including four husbands, her mom, her children, and a grandchild. Her modus operandi was arsenic poisoning.

She laced her victims' food and drinks with the lethal chemical and watched while they convulsed and died. Arsenic poisoning imitates stomach cramps and general illness, so it was almost the perfect crime, except the police caught on when husband number five "mysteriously" passed away. The detective ordered an autopsy and found his system

217

full of enough arsenic to kill 20 men. Following this discovery, the bodies of her past victims were exhumed, and it turns out they all had arsenic in their systems. She got the nickname "Giggling Granny" because reportedly, during her interview with the police, she couldn't stop laughing. She giggled throughout her entire confession, after which she stated, "My conscience is clear."

Katherine Knight

Katherine Knight was no saint. She already had a track record of insane behavior long before she committed her most famous crime. She tried to strangle her first husband, attempted to kill her newborn baby, slashed a woman's face, and kidnapped a young boy. She eventually met and married John Price, a father of three. After discovering her mental instability, he took out a restraining order. However, he apparently couldn't resist her sexually, and still invited her to spend the night. That night would be his last. She stabbed him to death over 37 times, beheaded him, and draped his skin over a coat hanger. When his mutilated and skinned body was found on the living room floor by the police, it was reported that his head was boiling on the stove, parts of his butt were cut up, and stir-fried on the stove. Katherine was sentenced to life in prison without the possibility of parole in 2001. She is currently serving her sentence.

So again, there's a huge difference. Don't get it confused. They have very little in common. A lot of people just don't know the definition of these words, nor have some even thought about what is what. You gotta ask yourself if you can honestly handle the beast that I am. Can you really take on the challenge? Do you believe you can overcome it? Are you strong enough to get through to the end? Are you mentally and emotionally capable of trying to understand who I am and try to show me another lane?

The first step is knowing what you're up against so that you can understand what you are facing. Make sure you can ignore the mean lashes that can be dished out if it comes to it. You gotta play it out like Beauty And The Beast was played out. There's always a spot in the heart that can be touched in the beast and in any monsta, trust and believe.

Chapter Twenty - Three

Trapping Doesn't Work

I believe that y'all females like to try everything possible to trap a hustler. I don't care what type of hustle it is, whether in the streets or going after a career. One thing about you once you get in your feelings you're in them. It seems like you become someone vindictive. Especially when you know we are just friends, or when you feel I am on the verge of leaving you. You have to ask yourself why we are just friends at that time. Is it a work in progress? It is something you needed to do that you're doing wrong?

Again, you never want to pressure a man just because you're ready.

Why can't I be on the verge of leaving? What did you do? Can it be fixed? Yes, sometimes it can be two dudes you are dealing with that just want to be single for life or whatever, but sometimes it's y'all that ran us away. There's something that can be fixed and some things you just gotta let go of. You can't force a man to be with you. I don't move by force. It only makes me stand on my decision even more on whatever I decide. Sometimes prayer can be one of your choices before you start getting out of hand.

I wonder how many of you reading this can guess where this is leading to. I bet if you're right, it's only because you or someone you know or maybe even heard that it has been done. A lot will be in denial and will not confess or admit. They do not, or you do not want to seem crazy, but it's facts. Why do you feel if you get pregnant or have a man's baby, he's locked in with you? Believe it or not, y'all think that by doing so he's going to do the honorable thing and be with you, and y'all will be one big happy family. You feel he's stuck, and no one's going to want him since you're pregnant, but that's not the case. You got to be careful who you have a baby for and try to log in. You might lock in somebody you don't want once he shows his true colors. Be careful what you ask for.

I know a lot of y'all can relate to what I am saying, ain't that right? You're probably asking yourself how it is a traffic jam if it takes two. Well, because you say you don't want any kids, and I haven't any or any until marriage. Some of y'all say you're not having any unless he's the one you're going to be with. So, just as much as he is not using protection, you are not using protection, and if the condom does come off, you allow it. You say you're good on kids or whatnot and that you'll never trap him, but in your eyes, I bet you do. You're going to say, why have sex if you don't want kids? I both agree and disagree with that statement.

I believe, if 100 women have their partners use the male condom, but they don't use it correctly every time, at least 18 women will become pregnant in a year. If your partner uses a condom and pulls out before he ejaculates — comes — then you're using two different kinds of birth control methods. The webmd.com states that each year, 2 out of 100 women whose partners use condoms will become pregnant if they always use condoms correctly.

What are the odds of getting pregnant with a condom? It is stated on plannedparenthood.com that if used correctly, male/external condoms can be up to 98% effective at preventing pregnancy. In reality, they are only 85% effective – an average of 15 people out of 100 get pregnant when using condoms as their only form of protection for a year. Did you know sperm can leak out the base of a condom? It sounds like it's possible that some sperm leaked out of the condom and into your vagina. That's because the penis goes soft after ejaculation, which makes it harder for the condom to stay on and easy for semen to leak out. Emergency contraception is more effective the sooner you take it. So it's not always the man's fault as sometimes it's the fault of all that extra added shit that comes with sex.

If it's neither of our fault if it happened, so it's like why go through it? Yes, I can read y'all mind now with the extra stuff saying that it was meant and so on and not believing in abortions. So basically, a man has neither say nor feelings. The woman holds all the power. Now the situation turns sour if he doesn't want it. You force him into something he does not want and now he's hoping to God it ain't real. I feel like giving him the option to say he wants it or don't want it. Let him give his opinion as a man. Maybe he's fine with having the baby or maybe he's not but to don't take that input from him .

Why have a child from a dude that wishes it's not true nor his? Knowing he's praying it's not cuz he doesn't want it? Now you're bringing a child into this world knowing that the father is wishing a negative outcome about the child. Then in a way you keeping the child is now forcing him to be a father. Now you have to live with knowing it's not genuine at all. You probably thought he would change his mind or even be around.

I feel y'all be scandalous and conniving because y'all have the power to then do this child support shit, it's entrapment in my eyes. Now you feel you got me by the balls to rethink the whole situation and it's cheaper to be with you. He's just a sperm donor. You got the sperm from a sperm bank. As a matter of fact, you wanted another person to take full responsibility for a decision you made on your own. I don't know. Maybe it's just the way a thug looks at it. Call me what you want. I'm just keeping it real that's all.

I feel if a man is placed on child support, the woman should be responsible for half so that it's not just her sitting around collecting. I believe child support shouldn't be paid. I think it should be things that need to be paid. School supplies and clothes should be given if needed, not money. If it's sports or something, both parents should have to put forth half, and a letter from the school should be given saying it's been paid for that specific child.

For medical reasons, both parents pay, but no money should be given to her because I believe 90% of the time, it's not used for childcare. It is used for her own personal use with no proof it was a use for the child. Sometimes the money is used for her other kids that have nothing to do with my responsibilities. Granted, some dudes are lame as hell and just dipped out. I feel it's a difference. I know only 37% would agree on what's being said, but y'all will mainly be on your defense of understanding and argue the hell out of what's being said right now.Not too many will keep it real, but it's all good. It's normal for y'all to be one-sided fa real fa real.

I think there's a good lesson and this is not really a negative or less necessarily negative. I think knowing this gives you clarity on what and how we feel and why you should take better and more precautions before getting in that situation. I feel you should be extra protected. Be sure of whenever you do and y'all agree on something. Don't just be ratchet as hell and try some bullshit.

Believe it or not, some women are super ratchet, have kids for taxes, and for other dumbness. They'll have a child just because they know they can get some money out of to do the dude cuz he might have some money. So sometimes, you do it in faith of him staying or money. Okay that's what y'all wanted. Just make sure to make the right decision. Some of y'all are down right bad. Y'all can't pay your bills now and you are about to have a child. That's crazy, right? It's because y'all feel maybe he's going to give y'all the extra money for the child. Believe it or not, some of you truly believe that nonsense for real. Sometimes they don't work out the way you think. Please know that also. Trapping doesn't always work.

Chapter Twenty-Four

Fallin' in Love

Falling in love can be good and it can be bad for real. I don't think it's always a good thing to be in love, maybe more towards the good side, but yeah. I think for a thug, it is different, so I will explain it the best way that I know how to. It's is very confusing to me. I don't even realize when I am in love at that time. I feel like I just mess with you the long way. Like we just close as hell, and we got each other back. It ain't no secret we grew tight as hell. I think we don't realize what world we crossed into.

Experiencing this thing called love can be different and definitely feel out of the norm. Especially for a gangsta like me. When I start to notice myself getting that uneasy feeling, I quickly ask myself what in the hell is going on. I start saying some stuff that I normally wouldn't say and I feel like I am getting sensitive on a few occasions. That's not the type of stuff I be on for real. I don't really like it at all. I'm gangster! I'm not supposed to be having feelings and emotions as such. That's for y'all that mushy sensitive stuff. I look in the mirror and tell myself "Tighten up! Man up! What are you doing?"

I feel like I'm slipping on life. Like I'm spending too much time with you. Sometimes I wake up in the morning and realize and I've been laying up for days and haven't been on the block getting to that bag. The homies hit me up trying to figure out what I got going on period. Making me realize I am getting soft as hell, and I'm on a leash or something. That further makes me realize that I was right. I need to tighten up to get back to my normal self.

Like it's crazy because I'm a street dude. So I need to be in the streets. If I'm laid up I'm not getting things done, and that's not good. I got too many that depend on me, my leadership, and at the same time there's a bunch of people that's happy they don't see me on the Block at all. They can hustle up when I am absent. So, I definitely can't be on a leash and laid up in the house. I gotta keep that pressure in the streets. It's crazy, though because the weirder our relationship becomes, the more I find it to be your fault. I'm against it really. I enjoy it slowly, but surely, I still check myself. The homies tell me I'm changing on them and they feel like I'm falling back. And this could bring problems whether you think about it or not. Sometimes the homies you have can become jealous not in that homo type of way but just a sense of losing a best friend. Being jealous that you're changing on them for a female like it's been us as a family before her.

I'm spending more time with you and than being on a block getting money, doing what we do to get a bag, being with other females, or building a million-dollar operation we always dreamed of having. And see once there is jealousy, there is envy and negative energy towards you as the woman. Those thoughts are never good at all at that point. They start a subplot on you and may not always be to harm you, but it may be to get you out the picture.

They don't have a problem with y'all doing what y'all do. But when

I start to slip and get too caught up and, the money slows in the street and it starts to come charging in. We got a code out here in the streets. It's three letters that represent three words M.O.B (Money Ova Bitches). That means no woman comes between this bag, friendship, or bond. And at this moment I am starting to break the code. It is a violation of our bond. See it's bigger than what you may think. It's not just saying words that have no weight. It's like violating a game that you're in by wearing them. Opposite color knowing that's against cold unless there is a presentable X on whatever it is that you're with that indicates no disrespect to the team is just something that goes with what you're wearing. Being in love causes me to have to go against the code and the homies in some way.

Well, it really depends on what type of woman you are because if you are with the streets that means you're not going to try to keep me locked down. In fact you're going to wake up and say, "Baby be safe out there get that bag." That's when you become like family to the home. Almost like 2018 Superfly. He was getting it and his women were getting it with him too. They were his ride or die; they were with whatever he was with and didn't cross their boundaries.

Most women try to change a man just like the man tries to change a woman by force. I am a little different because I am a provider in a mentally. When you met me I was in the streets hustling. I mean I still am. But you got to realize we don't like y'all try to change us. That just falls under being pressured again like you know I am a full-blown Street dude coming in this relationship and you liked it. Even if you're a good girl and you come in knowing who and what I was; respect it. I believe you deal with who you attract.

Meaning, if I met you in the club, I can't get mad when you're in the club cuz hell that's where I met you. If I met you in a church, I believe that's who you are. I don't care where that's a start of knowing something about you. If you meet me in a strip club don't feel some type of way when I still go to the strip club. I understand that change is good depending on the circumstance. I understand the whole being afraid of something happening, but this is what I do. I do this in my sleep for real. I see all the killings, people getting robbed, and so on. But I know what I'm about. Like I feel imma make sure I get my man before he gets me. Plus, I'm not into making enemies though sometimes they emerge from the darkness. More the reason I feel that I'm liking you is if you are changing my emotions; especially if it's happening fast.

There's good and bad that comes with falling in love for a thug. It feels like my soul has been snatched away from me with a blink of an eye. It feels like I've become someone other than myself. But then there's this crazy feeling like I've become less than a man because of falling in love. I said being sensitive and mushy. It just don't seem to me that no strong man should feel as such. Maybe I'm just so Thug and don't realize it's normal now to do so. I know true gangstas that were comfortable doing so that I can think of.

When I start feeling like I would rather be with you than to be out to me that's bad. I don't think that's the way it should go. I was told being mushy insensitive was being soft and female like. It was never okay to be nothing other than hardcore gangster. It depends on the type of woman you are when it comes to who I am and become. Cuz let's say you're a goody that sees a rose emerging from the concrete. Maybe you say, "I can change him." Let's say you start to slowly be successful in doing so. Hell I make so I can look at the streets and homie like it's no good for me. Are you going to stay for good or will I regret choosing you over my life?

Mind you I have no complaints out here, but wanted to be rich as Pablo Escobar. I'm in love with the streets already but I'm married to the game. That means you're saying you're going to be here through the bad and the good. Not only that but be my therapy. Spoil me. Take me places that streets could never take me. When I'm hungry you're going to feed me. When I feel lost you're going to find me. When I fall you're going to pick me up. If I get beef from the change you're going to ride and see me through. If I leave my life for you baby girl, that means there is no turning back. We are married without the valves. I'm not breaking up who I am for no temporary waste of time.

Be careful what you ask for when you ask or try to change me. Let me change on my own time or just don't choose me to be the one you come for. There's bad and good with me falling in love with you. Cuz I take trust and loyalty to heart it's not a game. I tell you I love you is deeper than the ocean. But falling in love can have me crazy as hell. I will be ready to punish anybody that steps in the path of us or come between us. I could perform actions that would have me looking insecure. Questioning these dudes look at him speaking to you. The dudes you work with or friends. I'm looking at them strange now. You got to realize though this is new to me.

I'm used to chilling, sex and I'm looking out for you when I can. I'll see you when I see you type of relationships. That went from that to staying together. Having sex every single day and seeing you every day of course. The sex is crazy as hell you be putting on a performance acting bad with it. You know how to snatch a man's soul from him, you cook your ass off, you're super sexy, and cater. This is nothing I can just accept and convert over to doing. I got to adapt. It's bad enough I'm still trying to break down what's happening but it will happen.

The feeling is crazy like I feel like you put a curse or some type of roots on me. Like I'm under some spell. I swear y'all got bones in your socks LOL, for real. I understand though. They say there's always one that can get to your heart and change you. Yes, women love harder but we take falling in love differently it's actually scary, real talk. Again, I'm not into being out here securing the bag and all of a sudden start to feel myself miss you. That shit is very awkward all that is crazy to me. Me?

Icy Gucci Mane and Keyshia Ka'Oir have the best relationship. They share a love I see that Ghost and Tasha share love it's a street love. I see us building an empire like Cookie and Luscious Lyon. I'm still doing what I love and you're with whatever I'm with. Whatever I decide you got my back; no ifs, ands, or buts about it. The feeling of being in love is the biggest emotion you ever experienced; next to losing a loved one. It's a feeling that's not easily revoked. Sometimes we may not want it, sometimes we may be too impractical.

Do you want to know a secret? Ladies, I'm trying to help. That is why I say things as such. But gangsters are scared of falling in love and also afraid to be hurt, especially about women. A man goes through more trauma when it's a woman that breaks his heart. The first one we fall in love with is our moms. Sometimes she breaks our heart first which can make us bitter towards women. Like we become nonreactive to falling for another woman. And it's hard for us to forgive you once you break our hearts.

It's crazy how you can forgive the worst of the worst that a man could do but we can't. Really I can't really tell you why we can't. It's not by choice all the time sometimes. It's just instilled into us from birth. You are naturally a forgiver. You do it even when you don't understand why. Maybe it's because you're in love and you accept the emotions and feelings you go through from falling.

How does falling in love feel? It feels like I'm losing my breath sometimes. I think when we get on y'all for being out or going too long it's maybe because we miss you and want to know if anybody is trying to steal you away from us. It feels like finding someone you've been looking for all your life. Like I did some more Forrest Gump shit and ran across the world to find you just to catch up. I'm onset Thug Love and it's not just represent for sex it's a way of loving someone deeply than the norm. It's just more on the tougher side. It has everything falling in love has, but more on the street side. It's hard to explain really. I will be like Cain and Jada or Menace to Society. He loved her but still loved the streets along with his love for her. I would go dumb about you with no hesitation.

There's good and bad with falling in love with you. I believe falling in love will make me even crazier than I am now; true story. There will be no limit. I will go to make sure we good. I would seriously hurt somebody if they disrespect like Cain did in the movie . See when you dealing with me you got to realize off top I'm no joke. I'm not going to play with nobody when it comes to mine. What's mine is mine. I will tolerate no disrespect especially if you done made me fall and this thing called love. Can you really imagine how I'm coming when it comes to you?

Why do you choose me? I ask again because you could choose the good dude. I am a straight street dude. I don't look to ever fall in love and put you before my money. Why wake up a monster. I mean, yes, I'm already that. That's what I hear. But why take that chance and make me fall deep? Is it the challenge? Is it because you're intrigued by who I am and where I come from? Is it because you like bad boys? Do you want to be a bad girl? Do you think it's just super sexy? Is it because of the money? Is it because I'm street or book smart with it? Does it start by you just wanted to have sex out of curiosity to see what it would be like? But you end up getting locked in?

I think it is better for you to let me do me and come when I'm ready. I had a woman I was with tell me no matter how mad she was at me she still wanted me under her. I don't think it's healthy for a man to be up under a woman all day every day. I don't think it's healthy. For either side to do that, for real. You'll begin to see things in each other that you didn't before and feel some type of way about it. I think after a while you would. We would get tired of it and begin to need space. At least if we both got things to do. It'll give us time apart. When I am on the block all day you'll be able to do what you do. There is a such thing as too much time together. In fact, you should be encouraging me to go out and get money whatever way I am. No man should be laid up like a woman with nothing to do with no type of job.

I am in search of loyalty more than commitment because I believe loyalty will be there no matter what takes place between us. I feel like this relationship thing is overrated and not of the norm anymore. From what I have seen, there's not many successful relationships that last over five years and even more rarely ten. I've always said it's not like it used to be back in the day. Let's both fall in love with loyalty. I can deal with that instead of all that extra mushy stuff. I feel like you should do it at your own risk. So take the good with the bad and whatever else if you choose to continue on.

Chapter
Twenty-Five

My Loyalty

As I've always said, the two most important things to me in any type of relationship is trust and loyalty. Those two things take you to places you only dreamed of going. It'll put you around people that are in the highest areas you never stood next to. Gaining my trust and showing me that you're loyal can make me fall in love faster than anything; it'll make me feel some type of way. I understand since I am a thug, I am always in the streets, and there's a lot of hearsay. The project streets be joking about how a thug will never settle or hold his women down.

So, I know women are going to say we probably wouldn't be loyal in a relationship. And y'all automatically assume we are "hoes" just because hoes be in our face, in your words. I do not understand this. How are you saying anything when you don't know anything about what I do.? Even if you did hear it I've messed with someone or or two people that don't make me a hoe. I know that is disloyalty. If I am single and I'm out here getting money, I can do what and who I please. What I do is no one's business to keep it G. Who cares who and how many females I do knock-off when I am single? You would have a better chance on being labeled a whore if you tried to do what I did and have sex with many people.

Whore: a person who thinks having sex with only one

person means one person at a time. (SD)

Can I still have sex with multiple people and thinks it's okay? You have a vagina and it becomes loosely shaped and becomes damaged goods. You smashing multiple dudes in your life will not be good for trying to find a husband. You ask me if I think only one woman can be labeled as that. You can tell by your vagina that you've been one. You can't tell by looking at our private area. That's just how I feel. Like you know it could damage you but you continue to do it. Can I be loyal? I can be very faithful in a relationship, but what do you mean by loyal? And what way is the question asked? If I'm a man in a relationship with you, I'm loyal to you. No one will ever come before you at all. You are what we call wifey in the hood.

Wifey: a real lady, not you're only, but your favorite different from the hood ratchets. Sexy in every way possible. When she smiles and even when she's mad at you, she is still sexy. (SD)

Well, she can have everything she wants. I would kill for her with no question. I will go over and beyond for my wifey; there's not too much I wouldn't do for her real talk. If I'm still in the streets and I mess around here and there but, home is always with wifey. And everybody knows that anybody I do deal with knows what's up. And again, I won't tolerate no disrespect. Point Blank. Believe that. It's not always like this. All of us mess around on our wifey. Some keep it 1000. There are some that will keep it real and tell you they like smashing different females sometimes. Depending on who you are you can kill that by being open to threesomes with him. Maybe you already understand how he is and you say don't make no babies or bring no disease home, and that I better keep whoever in check.

Right now you think I am crazy or lost my mind but believe it or not women do it. Not only do they but they like girls too and would rather pick the girl herself. And believe it or not these things do work. They are proven cuz now no man has a reason to cheat now. A lot of the time, well most of the time, there's no feeling between me and them females. I think what it is that we want to get some new sex because we want something we can prove to ourselves. It's like I'm done, I'm doing it for weeks because I don't have to prove myself no more. I am proven.

Maybe that falls under excitement. Maybe you got to just turn things up sexually. Maybe acting and role-playing; spice it up if you act as another woman something like a Jamaican England. Shit a white girl. It could stop us from going and playing around. A lot of things are all in the mind. You putting on a wig and changing your voice makes it seem to me as if you are someone different. Especially if you stay in character and help my big ass imagination see you as someone different.

Imagine this right. Imagine we are settled in or I come over and I come upstairs to the room. And you got on a wig and a sexy ass outfit. You start talking in another accent. And you say some shit like "Hey Daddy. Wifey is not here right now. I am house sitting for tonight." Then you continue to say, "How about we have some wild, crazy, sweaty sex" and at the same time grabbing my dick and hiking your breast up in my face. You know you got to sell this act and you can't fall off the stick with it. If you do this successfully I guarantee you I would be excited. You got to do things like this. If it's just the same old same old I will get bored as hell or just feel I need to smash something I want to prove myself to somebody. This is why we like dealing with a few because we won't get burnt out by the same stuff. It'll be different if I got wifey and maybe two others.

Women these days just believe from the back and me on top is all it takes. Well, some of y'all. See the others are different. One rides the horse like it's real. The other one is straight nasty. She gets it in with no chill out at all for real. Probably things you don't want to do or refuse to do that they will. There's always someone out there that would do everything you won't and it is something we don't want to let go of all for real for real.

In certain countries you're allowed to be married to two women at the same time. I wonder if we are just born that way, maybe one is not enough. Can I be loyal? Depends on what we talkin' about. You asking me if it's possible to actually be with one and only one. I feel I can do anything I set my mind to do. If I want to deal with only one I can, but the question is will you be the one that makes me want to? I think it depends on you; how you are coming and how you are bringing this statement in love. Are you going to make me feel like no one has ever made me feel? Are you going to remain that person when or if you do? Things tend to change once you win over the person you're pursuing. That plays a part in if I just be with you just because, or if I decided to give you my attention then you later turned sour. I can tell you I will probably go find that sugar I once had from the jump.

Will I ever settle down? Again that decision is in your hands. See, I don't care if we are just friends I feel you need to show me your traits. I need to see what I'll be getting and who I'll be settling down with. Y'all came to believe I shouldn't see that until I decide to settle. Well, why would I if you're showing me nothing at all. You're only showing me you can be no different from any other chick. So you don't stand out at all and if you think your vagina so good that's all you need you are sadly mistaken. If I'm dealing with different women, I guarantee they all got good snatch. Might have one that got some all right, but her head game is out of this world. Maybe she treats me like a King to make up for what she is lacking in others. You got to display your talents.

I'm not saying you got to show out but at least show up. If I go to a free martial arts class, they will show me why they are better than the rest. They will show me enough moves to suck me in. Then they'll show me everything else once I'm signing up. I need to see a movie with you and you only; when I got others that are going to get it poppin' in all types of different ways.

Will I ever settle? Depends on where I am in life. Once I get focused on something I am locked in. I need no distractions. I need to keep on my game face on. You will soon understand how locked in I am when it comes to my life and career goals. So if you decided to still pursue me that would only tell me you're not going to scare me away nor waste my time. One of my biggest fears is time wasted. If you come along and somehow get close enough to make me want to let you in, that means you gain some trust with me. Once you gain my trust, don't play and mess that up cuz.

If you betray my trust, it will never be the same again because I can trust you mentally but my heart can't. Once a man's heart is broken, there's really no coming back unless I so deeply fall in love and I can get pass this problem somehow. Can I settle down? Yes, but it takes some things to persuade me before I could consider it. If you're doing something that I love, you'll get me to settle down because I would not want anybody else winning you over from you wanting me.

All this ties into why we cheat. I mean I want excitement and to be stress-free. I don't want to go back and forth all the time. I know it's going to happen sometimes but not wanting to go through it often. That's why I was single when you met me. It was less stressful and I was obligated to no one to do anything. I didn't have to put up with absolutely nothing from no woman. When I am on my own quiet thinking time, I don't want to be bothered or feel pressured to tell you what's wrong. Sometimes, maybe most of the time nothing is wrong. I just want to be in my own world. Bothering me drives me crazy. It'll push me to the next woman.

Sometimes just give me a massage when you think I'm stressed or inside a different world instead of going on and on. Another thing, being lazy as hell during sex and all the whining when I'm going to toss you around and be strong will do it, too. That'll kill my vibe with you especially if I'm horny as hell. If you deny me sex and get moody all the time or stop taking care of yourself that causes me to cheat also.

My loyalty may have its question marks to you, but really there's no question. You want to know why I am always with the homies. I'm with them because it puts me in a different element other than that mushy stage. It keeps me on point. I done seen the ugliest dudes get soft and forget sometimes he's a King. Sometimes I want to talk shit to the homies, watch football, and work out at the gym lifting 400 lb. I'm with the homies cause we are out here getting to that bag. We are a mob. We get it together. We got each other's back.

So, yes, we are always together in order to be sure everyone makes it through the day to see another day. When no one else is there, including you, we will always have each other's back; we're family. We are more like brothers than homies. We are family and we were chilling and hustling way before you came in the picture. Not saying they will be forever in front of you or before you, but there's just levels to the importance of positions you all play in my life. I really don't want to be into comparing and don't ever want you to feel like you got to compete. Just like your homegirls.

They are your friends that were there before I was in the picture. I understand that. The problem only comes if they get to the point where they're talkin' shit about you or if they talk shit about me. That becomes disrespect. I need no one dictating nothing about my personal life. That is not acceptable by any means unless one of us was a no-good ass motherfuker to each other; flat out.

I think if you start to get too comfortable and start to slack off being on fleek because your mission has been fulfilled that could be a problem. As in getting me to be yours so now you don't feel you should have to keep yourself up; hair, nails and so on cause you feel you don't have to. You start looking like you don't care at all about what turns me off. So now when I see women that look how you used to do before this, it actually makes me aroused. Grab my dick and lick my lips cause I love bad bitches. I gotta a fuckin problem. I love that fleek shit that's what I was drawn to not that ratchet look.

Like I said before you got to stay on your shit messing with me. Not staying on your shit can make me attracted to someone who is. Let's say even more attracted, smh. See I can be attracted to her look or how she makes herself look and not react cause the ones that look like that sometimes have smelly flaws or maybe disfigured flaws so it's not always something that will make me react; trust me.

Now, there's some that don't care, but I'm a boss. You gotta be bad all around head to toe. Men don't just cheat. It's things that are occurring that influence us to say fuck it. Women seem to feel we just born cheaters and that's not true at all. Like it was said earlier in the book, sometimes we are provoked to do so. You get on me about being on the block or with the homies all the time that can be a problem. You get on me about not being up under you all day 'till you start asking and assuming that I am cheating. Now what if I'm not cheating? After a while it's like I might as well because you're already insecure as hell and continuously saying you know I am. If I'm going to be guilty before proven guilty I might as well do what I do.

Do I feel bad for cheating? That question depends on the situation. You got to really break down the levels of cheating. You got to define the relationship that you share with someone to even know if it's cheating. I know women that have someone that they having sex with exclusively because they don't want to have sex with others but they are just friends. But they also feel that I should be the same way when really that's not an obligation. Just because you feel as if you want one partner doesn't mean I want one partner. In the mind of a woman, she might feel like it's a form of cheating on her and you will know that because they'll get in their feelings once they find out that you're having sex with someone else other than them. But she continuously fail to realize that we're just friends and we fuck around the long way.

Do I feel bad for cheating? I mean yes. There could be times where I feel bad especially if we're together in a relationship. I mean it's not like I just want to cheat or I feel good about it. Sometimes I just feel home isn't the same once you're in a relationship or you get too comfortable being around each other. I feel like I want to feel like it's the first time we met as much as possible. I'm not set up to just bring harm and hurt to a woman's feelings because like I said before, a mother is a man's first love. So there's no way that I'm just hurting you or making you feel less than a human being. It's just who I am nothing against who you are.

I have a low tolerance level for things that are supposed to be simple but you just fail to do. Some things are common sense. Some things are just ridiculous and some women just can't get things right.

There are things as a woman you should know to automatically do, but I end up having to show you. I can't lie a lot of these dudes are the same way they're not man enough to understand certain grown man things.

If you go out with me on an all-expense paid trip, let's say to Jamaica, and it's for three nights; something to help us reset. Tell me, are you gonna enjoy every second and forget everything going back home for this time? Are you gonna enjoy the time and let nothing stop you from taking advantage of every second of those days? Are you gonna show appreciation for every second of the trip and make sure there's no dull moments? It's bad enough I'm not into this type of shit, and at the same time, my vibe gets killed fast because you are not being appreciative.

But why do y'all give off the impression that y'all aren't grateful and even trying to enjoy the gesture? Why should I have to make you enjoy us time? It's like y'all feel like somebody owes y'all the world. Or as if y'all don't want to be there and if so why come? You kill my vibe instantly with all that pouting for no reason "Oh I'm tired" or that"Ain't nothing wrong" shit .When clearly I'm lit and you're not. This is the reason I don't be on all this. Trying to do stuff with you, build something, shit. And then you kill my vibe and now you wanna get lit cause you're too far up your own ass to realize you killing the set.

Now you make me say to myself "I tried. I can't do this shit. It's not for me. I'm cool on this building further than friends shit with her." Now, I'm thinking of other people who would've enjoyed the gesture and who would've been lit 'til we boarded back on the plane to head back home. Now I start to realize even more why I felt like I never wanted to or wanted to go any further than what we had from jump. It makes a man wanna lay next to someone who will appreciate and take advantage of every second of time spent.

The sad part about this is this whole incident will get flipped on me by the end of the day. Why? Because women don't wanna take responsibility for their reactions. Like I said before y'all don't even realize what energy y'all giving off. And the second it's pointed out y'all don't believe it. It's like we're just making shit up just to make shit up. Y'all so deep in self. Y'all will think we just say things to ruin the moment. I can't say it's just women. Some of these dudes do it too, but not how y'all do it.

Sometimes you gotta listen because there's no way on God's green Earth you can't see outside of yourself and like it's impossible when it comes to seeing yourself. So, you can't tell people what they see is not possible. If they see it, they see it. That's just what it is. You either fix it or stay set in your ways. But when you do that, remember your gonna run off any good man you are gonna encounter.

Chapter Twenty-Six

Q & A Survey: Professional Vs. Thug

If my best friend was flirting or tried to give you sex, would you tell me and would you or would you do it?

Professional: I would definitely put her in her place first, letting her know that ain't real at all. And next time she tries it or steps past that boundary I will let you know. The only reason I won't just tell you off top because she's probably been your friend forever. And I don't wanna see hurt, pain, and anger in your heart. Plus, I can handle people when they need to place. But she only gets one time.

Thug: It depends what type relationship we got, fa real. And if you know how your friend is why have her around me? Mainly, If you and I just sexing, nothing more nothing less, I probably smash her, too. If I deal with you on a deeper level I would probably tell you yo' lil friend thotting. Ha! Probably just best to keep those types from around me real talk.

What are some experiences that made you who you are today?

Professional: Growing up watching my mother struggle to pay bills and feed us. Trying to keep myself in a safe environment. Seeing family and friends fight addictions and losing family and friends to death or the prison system. I feel like I've been through it all. Really not much to say I haven't experienced. The important thing is that I wanted and accepted change. Change for the better though. I decided to get some degrees under my belt and pursue a career. So I can get a paying job that'll definitely change the lives around me definitely mine.

Thug: Coming up during poverty and being misfortune. Didn't really wanna be home; to many people in one house was too much. Still going through the struggle and being head first in the streets. Kicked out from school for constantly fighting cause people talking shit about my family. Talking shit about the clothes I was wearing and still being smart as hell; grades speaks for itself. But I couldn't escape the streets seeing my family hurting and seeing homies dying out here; I wanted to get money. I saw the biggest dope dealers eating like rappers and I felt I needed to get there. So that's what I did. I went in with no emotions straight game face.

What do you consider a perfect life?

How would you make it work for me and you?

Professional: A perfect life to me is having everything that we need and being able to live outside of our means comfortably. A perfect life to me is this being happy with each other with little to no arguments. Perfect life to me is both of us on top of our game. Working good jobs and being able to have continued success. A perfect life to me is us going together conquering trust and loyalty and one day being together for the rest of our lives. A perfect life to me is letting no one be able to break our bond or come between anything that we built because what we share is more important.

It's not completely about how I will make it work for the both of us. It's about how we will make it work for the both of us. We are equal and shall remain equal. There's no one greater than the next. Our lives cannot be perfect if it's only me putting in the work; it takes two. Everything that we do to succeed I make our lives easier. Then our relationship grows which makes it perfect. The number one thing that'll make our lives more perfect or what I see as perfect is putting God first. An analogy that He is the way the truth and the light. I wish you would not not fall, because we should stand tall.

Thug: What I think it's a perfect life? I think a perfect life it's getting that bag till I can't no more. Not having to work for nobody; being my own boss. I want to be able to get whatever I want no matter the cost and whatever you want no matter the cost. We gotta get this bag together no ifs ands, or buts about it. We let nothing get in the way of our bag. We got to stay and stick together. We can't be beefing and going at it. There's a goal we got to meet. I think getting to this bag is a perfect life for the both of us because nothing can be done if you don't have a bag. It all falls back to that. So we can bet nothing will sidetrack us.

What do you think is my best quality and what attracts you to me?

Professional: I think the best quality that a woman can have is independence. Independence takes you a long way. It takes you further than your looks and your physical attributes. With independence I see intelligence, I see a go-getter. I see nothing stopping you from getting where you are trying to go. I see the strength in you. I see your faith in God. I see the faith that you have in yourself in the confidence to succeed and be great. I can see the woman second catering to a King. It shows why she can be his equal: half and half. There's so much that I see and there's so much that is important, but I think in order for us to grow and take over you got to be my Michelle Obama. You got to be able to get out there and do whatever you do. Be great at it. Because if I'm not around, you have to be able to hold it down with no problem.

I love that you have an open mind. I bet you're not judgmental. I love the fact that you are a fighter. You don't like giving up especially when you're in love. I love the fact that you're willing to change yourself and can adapt to whatever environment that you're in. I mean there's just so much stuff that I have to write about that. I would need another book to cover it. I love the fact that you believe in me and that you believe in my dream and that you're willing to back me up 100% and vice versa.

Thug: I think your greatest quality can be if you're an understanding type chick. Understanding my background or where I come from. Knowing I'm straight from the hood; from the streets. Knowing what type of man I could be and that I need a lot of work, but that it's going to take a lot of patience. Understanding that I've been to jail a few times and there's a chance that I could go back one day. Understanding that there is going to be upside down; good and bad. Knowing that you will stand loyal to me having my back no matter what. Understanding is high-quality. It's like one of the biggest qualities to have.

If your mother didn't like me or if we just had disagreements, whose side would you be on?

Professional: In this case it depends on whose wrong in the situation. It's not about whose side that I'm on it's about who's right and who's wrong. I know how some mothers are that don't like no woman that her son is with. And I understand that there will be indirect situations as such. By this time I'm probably used to my mama beefing with any women that's been in my life. So, I would definitely deal with it in that sense, but if you're wrong I will pull you to the side and have a conversation about the situation. If she's wrong, I will also pull her to the side. I want you to know that I have to pull the both of y'all together to let y'all know "Hey this is my mother for life and this is my woman potentially for life." So that means y'all would have to work it out. Because I can't have the two women in my life beefing.

We have to come together. You're my woman I'm going to stand up for you no matter what but its levels. I'll go to war with anybody in the world for you and if I can't go to war with them, I'll make sure that it works out where all parties are on equal grounds where no harm can come to you. I'm going to be your protector by all means but that doesn't mean that I'll go against my mother. If you're in the wrong, you have to understand that I will stand with my mother. If it wasn't for my mother, you wouldn't have me in your life right now even though it seems she doesn't want me in your life right now.

Thug: I can't go against my mom's because at the end of the day she's going to be there when you're not there. Sometimes you just have to be the bigger woman to understand that moms don't lose. I'll go up against anybody for you, but you can't ask me to go against my mother just so you can win and show that you're more important. My mother got my back and would do the same for me. Granted there are some mothers that put their husbands or boyfriends before their very own kids. I just need you to make my life easier and beefing with my mother is not going to help. I'm not going to let nobody just do you any type of way, but come on man, that's my mother. I wouldn't expect you to go against yours for me.

Do you want to have kids and when do you think is the best time for you to have kids?

Professional: I mean one day I would love to have kids, I would think. I'm not in a rush to have kids. I don't want to just have kids and not be financially stable. Even still I would like for it to be when I'm ready mentally. When I do decide to have kids, I would love for it to be when I'm ready. I don't want to have kids by accident. I want to make sure that the woman is who I'm going to be with; which I know is not of the norm anymore.

I believe 80% of people that have kids aren't with the person that they want to be with. It's always with the person they don't want to be with from a man's point of view. The woman may want to be with that person that they have the child with. But it's not always neutral. I do not want to be forced to have kids. I want it to be genuine. In another light, truthfully it's kind of contradicting because I look at it as it will be whatever God's plan is. I can't stop God's plan, but I would love it if He let it be my plan; how I see it for my life.

Thug: I'm not looking for any kids. I'm trying to get to this bag as normal. I'm trying to focus on myself and making life easier; much more lavish. So when I do have kids everything is A1. If I don't have kids, I'm not going to trip about it. I'm cool but if I do slip up then it is what it is. Just got to deal with it. I don't think there's a best time to have kids. I think you want to have kids. When you want to have kids, I think that is the best time whether you're rich or broke. It's whenever you're ready and you decide to want them.

How often do you expect sex?

Professional: I expect sex whenever I want it. I don't think there is a set number to how much sex or how often I want sex. There are times I want sex and there's times I don't. If I get aroused three or four days a week, five to seven days a week, or two or three times a day so be it. You just got to be able to hang. That's how I feel. Just as much as you want me to hang whenever you want it. A lot of women want sex all day every day and never get to the point of satisfaction. You got to think about it. What you don't do and won't do is when someone else will or would love to do it.

That's why it's good to stay in the gym. "Keep yourself in shape, get your sleep, take your vitamins, do everything that's needed to be healthy". Because with me, I don't care how sick I am, if I'm in the hospital, or in a wheelchair, if you want that D, you can get that whenever all facts. If a man is okay with just a few times a week, he probably got somebody on his team who is being real or getting ready to add somebody to his team. So you got to be ready. I don't care if you mad, happy, or sad when it's time to get down you gotta get down baby.

Thug: I want it every single day. I got needs. I need to get off to keep stress away. I've got to be able to look over and see you over there and get it when I want it. Don't matter if you sleep, or if you want when I want it. I want it. I don't think that you can really put a number on it. But I mean if I had to do it at least for five days a week, I can't say nothing less. I love sex. I don't think too many people don't like sex.

Who doesn't want to have sex every day? That sounds crazy not to have sex every day or at least a lot of times a week. I think it keeps down the tension and the arguments. Even if you have arguments I think it's the best makeup.

How do you practice faith?

Professional: When I am not at work, I do prefer to go to church and give God my time. But a lot of times I am working, so I just praise Him every day with prayer. I pray when I'm driving, in the shower, in the morning, and at night. I tried to spend time in His word as much as possible; with advice. But I also know it says I can give Him praise between any four walls. Whether it is in the bathroom, my bedroom, the living room, or the kitchen. We are the church. The people are the church. It's not the building. The building is just where we go and meet as a family; as a fellowship and give Him His praise. I also fast at times. I just don't do food. I fast from somethings that I feel like I need every day just to show Him and sacrifice that I love Him more than those things.

I put my faith in my trust in God Proverbs chapter 3 verse 5 & 6 says: "Trust in the Lord with all thy heart, lean not to thy own understanding. In all thy ways acknowledge him and he shall direct thy paths." The Bible also says I must have a mustard seed of faith and that can remove a mountain. (Matthew 17:20) So that's how I practice my faith. I never lose it. Never throw it away, and always believe nothing can change that. I build my relationship with God no matter where I am. It doesn't take me going to church.

Thug: I pray to God every day for getting me through these streets. He helps me get through crazy situations. Whether there are life or death issues I know it's Him that guides me through these streets, keeps me focused, and keeps me going. I don't go to church because I don't want to be a hypocrite. I know that I'm still out here thuggin' but I still know there's a higher power. I acknowledge that and I can't do it without Him at all.

Why do you feel like you lose when it comes to me?

Professional: I mean I feel like I lose coming into a relationship with someone with a past because whatever she has been through she automatically applies it to me. I feel like she starts to change her ways from her last relationship and the things that she used to do for her man. Some when I come alone she's bitter and sour towards a man. I have to take the consequences of her past. So to me it's like why date or try to let somebody into your heart if you're just going to make it to where I can't win.

I feel sometimes when you let go of a situation that caused so much pain and so much change you should let everything go with it. Don't carry over what was done in the past to the new. Remember, if you daydream about the past it pushes the future back. If you put me at fault for something that your past did, it may just run me away and you may miss your blessing. So when I got to hear about the bad things you've been through and why you don't do this and why you don't do that anymore. I kind of figure that either I gotta make up for everything that he did wrong. Or now I got to jump all these hurdles when I don't even deserve the consequences that he deserves.

This is going to make me stray away and feel like I'm weak because I didn't fight for you or I didn't want to put in the work. But you have to realize it's a difference when putting in work for what you want because you just don't want to give into me right off the bat. Then telling me I have to go all out to make up for all the BS you been through with your past relationships. That I can't do. That's not my obligation. That's not my job. That's not my fault and I will not make up for something that I haven't done to you personally.

Thug: I mean I feel like I lose when you start to get deep inside your feelings and forget what type of relationship we started. I know at this point it's going to be uncomfortable and I am going to feel obligated when I'm not supposed to be. It's hard to do what I want to do for you and not get you deep inside your feelings to where I feel obligated to do certain things for you. I mean I'm not really with that. I just want to stick to whatever agreement we have and whatever happens happen.

But the minute you start to get in your feelings, show it, become jealous, and so on that's when I lose. I either lose my mind or I feel like I lose a good situation that could lead to something good but detoured because you breached the contract.

If there is one thing in your past relationship that you could change, what would it be and why?

Professional: If I could change something in my past relationship it would be the communication. I think a lot of times communication strangles relationships and makes small things avalanches. I think a lot of things get twisted and misconstrued because of wording. One of the biggest things that can be chopped and screwed is text messaging. Text messaging can be taken however the receiver takes it and it may not be the way the sender sends it.

I realize no matter what, when I'm speaking to women my communication sometimes can be too strong and you can say I may forget or lose focus. She is soft, delicate, and just wants to be loved. I got to be gentle with her no matter what. She has feelings and is very sensitive; even if she doesn't want to be. I think that sometimes a man just has to be what we are accustomed to being and that's a punching bag. I see that to say we just gotta take what's dished out and let it roll off the chin. It's like we got to realize that it's a lose-lose situation because no matter what it will be flipped on us.

Either we could sit there and say,"Hey, Imma take these punches" or we can keep on moving and let her find a different punching bag that will maybe accept it. As for a real professional man, like myself. He'll handle business the way it's supposed to be handled. I'm not going to stand to be at fault to make you happy. You got to be responsible for your actions and acknowledge your fault.

Thug: If I had to change something, I think it would be our sexual encounters. Only because I don't know how to be regular in the bedroom. I tried to be the best that I can be every time and I know that is one of the reasons why you fall so deep and breach the contract. I got to take fault for my actions. I can't just place all the blame on you.

I think sometimes you just got to be regular whack you don't always want to have to go in hard and prove a point. I believe sex alone can change a lot of stuff and it's nothing to play with. I've seen lives being taken over some sex. I've seen the worst of the worst, it's not a pretty picture. Got to be careful on how and what you do, especially if you're not on the same page as that person but it feels like you giving off that impression.

Why are men so timid when it comes to moving in with us?

Professional: I wouldn't say that it's just privacy, but it's a mix of a bunch of things. I believe once you move in together there's no room for missing one another. I think that once you move in with each other you'll quickly start seeing little things that you don't like that'll become big problems. I believe it's good when you live in different spots. So you can always be able to go and clear your mind; reset. Plus, it's like we're both going to have our own sets of rules on how we feel we like things to be. For example, I hate getting up and seeing hair all in and on the sink; clean up after yourself. I don't want to wake up in the morning to a kitchen sink full of dirty dishes and the sink holder up when they are supposed to be down. Neither do I want to cuddle every single night. I hate when women get into bed with scarves or wraps on their head. I don't like the feeling. Another thing, I hate being in the bed under the blanket and there's loose hair all over it. I don't want to be questioned about anything. I want to come in at whatever time I choose to come home from work; I may be working late, etcetera. It's just a few things why we are timid on moving in together.

Thug: I mean I don't have too much of a problem with it if we're together. But can you handle me being in the crib bagging up these drugs? Can you handle me sitting in the kitchen for hours counting up money or maybe preparing the drugs for distro? Can you handle my gun being in the house on GP to make sure we good and safe at all times? Or will I hear about this every single day? Hear you nag me out every single day. Are you going to be preaching to me every day to change and leave the streets alone; when you already know how I am? I think this is a question you have to ask yourself. Also, are you truly ready for this?

How would you feel if you heard or found out that I cheated on you?

Professional: This question can be answered in a few ways depending on the guy. I believe in God so I do believe in forgiving but most men can't forgive it even once. Honestly, I don't know how I will feel because at that moment it wouldn't be clear-headed. You have some men that are so deep in love that they'll forgive you for it and continue on. Me? I don't know if I could bounce back from that. I know what type of man I am. I'ma give my all in a relationship. I got every area covered, especially sex that's not a problem. If you go out and cheat, maybe that's just who you are.

That automatically kills trust and loyalty once we are in a relationship. There's no breaking off I unless we agree upon it. For me the question would be "Why get in a relationship if you feel you're going to cheat?" We could just stay as friends, deal, not have those problems, and you can do whatever. If I chill down with you and get into a relationship, that's saying that I am dedicated to you and only you. I would not allow anyone or anything to break that bond, including cheating. You never know though. Anything could happen. You would truly have a lot to go through to get me back if it was possible.

Thug: It depends on how we are dealing. If we're together on the level for real for real, I'ma cheat on your ass back. An eye for an eye, right? I'm a probably fuck your best friend that been wanting to fuck me all this time. I probably still get missing on you like I said it just all depends. But don't think I ain't going to get my get back though; facts.

How long do you hold a grudge?

Professional: It depends on the situation. Like I said in the last question. I'm a man that believes in God's Word so I do forgive. But thoughts and memories can't just be erased. The things you do can't be erased, but it can be forgiven. If you did something real foul or something real ridiculous, it will probably be something that would last a long time. If it's something that's not too serious; probably within hours or maybe just the next day, as long as I speak my peace and let whatever problem I have be known and it gets handled I'm good. For the most part, I try not to let things linger on my mind and get the best of me or get to me.

Thug: Again, it depends. Really because if it's not too serious I'll laugh it off. In fact, for real, I really don't pay things attention if it's not too serious. If it's something that I don't like or feel needs to be tightened up I speak on it. I don't really hold a grudge unless it's something that doesn't get handled. But if you ever get me to the point where I look at you as somebody on the streets, and you do something to me the grudge might be forever. Just got to be careful on how you move and how you speak and that's facts.

Would you ever hit a woman?

Professional: I would never just hit a woman. I would leave before I get to a point of wanting to put my hands on her. Now, I will say this, if you try to harm me or my family, in any way physically, there's a problem. At the same time, I feel a woman shouldn't put their hand on a man either. My mother told me if a woman hits you, hit her back. I think if you don't want to be hit by a man don't put your hand on a man. There are some guys that just think they can put their hands on a woman when they want to and that's some bitch shit. I feel we should both be adults and keep our hands to ourselves and not react out of anger.

Thug: It all depends on why I feel I need to put my hands on you. I don't look to put my hands on you, but if you do something disrespectful or something harmful to me then it's on. I may not put my hands on you with my fist but I might grab your ass up. I think sometimes y'all need to be grabbed up a little bit because if you don't your cross boundaries.

What are your limits on sex?

Professional: If I got to tell you my limits on sex, that mean I shouldn't be with you. You should already know what my limits are off top. I'm game for whatever as long as you don't play me and no homosexual or disrespectful way. If you think about anything that's unusual that's outside of that you may need to ask me also before doing so.

Thug: Whatever you think my limitations are, stay away from it. If you're unsure about it stay away from me. That's all I really got to say.

Don't make this be one of those cases where I do got to put hands on you.

If I wanted you to go in the anal, how would you feel about that and would you?

Professional: I mean that will be on you. If that's something that you want to experiment with or it's something you like it is what it is. I think this can only be a weird question to a man if they don't know they're a man and they got some sugar in the tank. But I think some men have a problem with it at first because I grew up thinking that shit was gay. But as I went on through life I realized it's gay; if it's the same sex. So if that's what you

want; so be it.

Thug: NAS said,"Hit her where she dooty at / make her booty phat…" Ha, shit let's get it that's on you, frfr. It doesn't disrespect me in no way.

Why does a man like head(oral sex) so much?

Professional: I mean when I get head I just feel like a King. I feel Superior. It's nothing like seeing a beautiful face between your lap. To look down and see a woman on her knees pleasing a King just makes me feel greater than any other man on Earth. I think it's my high. It makes me feel like I do anything and it makes me feel like I'm loved and appreciate it. If I had to choose I would definitely choose head over penetration at that moment, but I still love penetration because that's what I get off with. Like I can't have sex with no one if they're not giving me head it's a must.

Thug: I mean what can I say. It's a wonderful feeling. It just feels so damn good. It's like giving my dick a massage. I love massages and my muscles need to be massaged.

Has a woman ever made you cry?

Professional: Only woman that ever made me cry was my mother...

Those ass whoopings hurt LOL!!!

Thug: Yea my grandma died on me. I cried like a baby real talk.

How do you feel about us sleeping at
your crib sometimes?

Professional: It's cool sometimes. I'm not against it. There are things that I don't like that make me not like it though. I hate when you leave stuff at my house because I don't leave stuff at your house. I don't like for you to have to use my brush, comb, and my clothes cause you didn't bring your own. I don't want to go in my bathroom and see hair all on and in my sink or if you act nosey as hell. Basically, it's similar to the question about living together.

Thug: I'm not tripping. Just act right. Clean after yourself and don't go looking through my stuff...... Don't touch my drugs nor my money or there's a problem.

How important is the word RESPECT to you?

Professional: Respect is very important because if you don't have respect for me I look at that as a term of "Fuck you." If you don't respect me, I can't trust you. I can't respect you. I go to distance for respect. I will not stretch the distance trying to prove myself to somebody for respect. I mean self-respect. Respect me as a man and what I shall receive. I will not be disrespected. There's consequences behind disrespect.

Thug: I'll die about it... Period.

Do you think of consequences first

before your actions?

Professional: I think that depends on the situation. Reactions are automatically in your brain when you're acting upon something and what could happen. Like if something went on with a family member where someone hurt them. If they were to call me that means I am the last resort. I'm coming with no question. I don't care about nothing at that moment. I'll deal with it later. But if I'm planning to do something, that means I'm taking time to think about what I'm planning. I know the positive and negatives about it. I'll have a good understanding of what could happen if I did follow out that plan. I just think it depends on the severity of the situation; if it's a life-or-death or if it's something that came up as an emergency right at that moment.

Thug: I think it's some situations. Sometimes the actions come before thinking about the consequence. Maybe I'll think about the consequences before my actions and sometimes that lead to me not carrying out that action. I try to think about the consequences first so I can be mentally prepared in case the consequences do come about. But sometimes it's just go time and you got to deal with consequences at another time.

Why are y'all so mean to us?

Professional: I don't think that I'm mean. I think sometimes mean gets mixed up with being honest. The truth hurts and sometimes comes out as mean, but really it's just what is the truth. I think y'all call us mean just cause we're not sensitive and emotional like you are. We start out as nice as gentlemen about something, but as time passes and something that we don't like continues our response is a little bit more aggressive. I am only mean when you take me to that place where I got to be mean.

Thug: I'm not mean. I'm just me. I guess I come off as mean, if that's what you call it. Then yeah, I am mean. I just don't take anything and don't like playing games. That can make me mean. Sometimes I feel like it don't matter what we do. We are always going to be mean. It is what it

is.

If we decided to do something freaky and record on your phone, would you show your friends and why do y'all like doing it?

Professional: Na, I'm cool on that. I don't show my friends any of my stuff. I don't get it on all that bragging stuff. I've been doing this. I don't need no player points. I think them dudes that ain't used to having player points are not used to having a badass female on their side do stuff like that. I'm definitely not sharing no female that I'm messing with the long way with the homies. Now, if you just a thought or something maybe, but even still I don't be showing off my business. I just don't rock that way. I don't need to be in the video showing the homies my package on the screen. Na, I'm cool.

I like the recording a video things for my own entertainment. I'm not into porn because I'm not into seeing dudes private parts all over the screen. I don't think no man should watch man on woman porn. If watching a dude's D in another woman mouth or coming in and out of her vagina turns you on, that's gay. Sometimes I want to look back when you're not on the other side of the bed or when your mad and I might want to do my thing and watch it.

Thug: If you my lady, I ain't showing nothing. You not about to be slobbering all over my girl. If she a lil hood star though that's different, haha. I'm probably not the only one with a video anyway. I like it cause I always wanted to do some type of porn, even though I don't watch it. I love seeing myself. It's hilarious I be trippin, but I don't really know why I do.

Why is it so hard for a man to be honest?

Professional: I don't think it's hard for a man to be honest. I just think that he has a deeper side that has a little sensitivity. He cares about you more than you think. That's why he's not honest about things and that is why I speak about that in this book. I can be brutally honest sometimes but when I do I will be looked at as a horrible type of man. I know for me and my type I could keep it 1000. Can you handle it and what would be next? Can we get through whatever it is or are you just going to penalize me for being honest? I don't think a lot of women can't handle the truth. They say they want the truth but just can't handle it. I know a lot of women that just rather not know. So, you gotta ask yourself.

Thug: I mean I don't know. I mean when we do dirt, of course, we don't want to get caught. We try to keep our dirt away from home and away from you. We're not just trying to straight out disrespect you and let it be known whatever it is. I mean, but at the same time, I really don't care. I try to have a heart when it comes to being honest with you. Like for me don't ask me if your cat stank because I may just give you the honest truth. But when I do all you're going to say is "You got me f'd up!" Sometimes it's just like why be honest if you're going to keep flipping it, it's turning me out to be crazy.

Why do y'all pretend not to care then show or express how you feel when it's too late?

Professional: A lot of men wear their emotions on their sleeves and it just doesn't come out how yours would. Our emotions are more bottled up. You can't expect the man to express how he feels like how you express it. It's two different outcomes of life. Sometimes we don't know how to show our emotions without feeling like we're mushy or soft. Sometimes it takes us time to show and express how we feel about you.

If it's rushed or we feel like we are pressured to show it, it gets buried even more. Sometimes when it's too late in your eyes that's a form of pressure and forcing us to come out right at that moment. Women always want men to have patience with them, but women don't want to have patience with the man. Don't always expect a man to respond how you respond to things that's not how it works. We come up harder and tougher. We don't know that soft side sometimes it has to be taught. To you, it may seem that it is a pretend. To us, it's not pretending. We just show it the best way we know how.

Thug: I mean it could be that I don't care at the moment. It could be things that happen between us can make me feel like I don't care. Maybe, it didn't hit me until I realized that you will walk out of my life; if emotions started to spurt. Why do you think there's a saying that says,"You never know what you have until it's gone?" Sometimes you don't know until that day comes how would I know if I don't get to that day? It takes a test to trigger those different emotions.

So, at that time, it can be that it's too late that could very well be one of those times that trigger my emotions. Or sometimes I flat-out don't care but I still have a lot of deep feelings for you and your well-being. Oftentimes, we don't know how deeply you hurt until that day comes to where you feel you want to walk out. That could show us that maybe we went too hard.

Why if you got a good one at home, doing everything going above and beyond, guys still seek more outside the relationship?

Professional: I think it goes back to what I said in the book where we feel we want to have to prove ourselves. It's just the urge of wanting something new and that new equals proven yourself. I think sometimes you just got to spice it up and do something out of the norm; a lot. Sometimes what you get so used to makes you feel like "Okay, I'm used to that I need something different." But then at the same time, a lot of men don't appreciate a good woman and don't know how to appreciate a good woman.

In my opinion, it's passed down from his father; watching how she did his father. I think men are just so used to ratchet females or hood-type females that when they get a good woman they it's not enough for him. It's like he wants her to be a good woman and at the same time I want her to be a ratchet ass woman. Men are just confused creatures; sometimes I'm not afraid to say that. We just don't know what the hell we want and that's not a good look. Me though? I can handle a good woman like that. I can't speak for the rest of the dudes really.

Thug: I think a lot of times we just not ready for a monogamy relationship. It's like being in the candy store. You see, so much candy that you want to eat and just don't want to choose one piece. I mean don't get it twisted. I can conquer anything and stay home to a good woman. But if she lacks streets smart, maybe that's why I'm kind of drawn to some outside influence. I like a chick with a rough side. If she doesn't have a rough side; it's like she's missing something. I'm a street dude, so it's only right that my woman has a little of that in there if not it's like I'm drawing to go get some. That's not always the case;

it's just like an example of one reason. But for real for real, I like having a good woman myself I think it's just mostly temptation that gets us.

What are two or three most valuable things in your life?

Professional: one of the most valuable things in my life is God; to be in His presence. Without God, nothing else can be important. Nothing else would matter. So, I probably wouldn't have life to be able to say those things are important. God is the most important thing a person can ever have. Secondly, I would like to say family. Family is very important because those are the ones that are going to be there when no one else is. Well, supposed to be there when no one else is. Last but not least my intelligence. A lot of people may say money is important, but you can't get money without intelligence. At least I feel like, if I got intelligence that brings money because I have the smarts to be able to go and accumulate.

Thug: I will say my money, my family, and my gun. I got to be able to protect myself to continue to live. With these three things I think I'm at peace. I feel better about things.

How do you feel about women asking men to marry them?

Professional: I mean what can I say. Go for the Gusto if it's something that you want and need; go for it. I don't think that you should let something go if you want it because you believe in some tradition. Because you feel like you're too good to do something. If you want to date somebody holler at him. You want somebody's number go get it. Sometimes you gotta be the aggressor when it comes to certain things, but only at times where it's not pressure full force. I mean, I've always seen men propose to women, but if he means the world to you it's important that sometimes you got to change the tradition; can't follow the trend of how it's supposed to be. Don't be afraid to let that person know how much you love them. If y'all on that type of level.

Thug: I mean, I ain't really thought about marriage really. I don't know if I'll ever be married. I just don't know. I've always seen different scenarios where men do it. And they do it however it feels special to them. I haven't seen too much of when a woman does it. So, I guess it will be on the guy to do it. I mean if she just feels the need to want to be with me for the rest of her life, that's how she expresses it, go for it. I can't really judge a guy because a woman proposes to him. How can you judge somebody that may not be ready or may not know how to propose. If she beat him to the punch; so be it.

If we get together, but I have kids by somebody else, how do you feel about that? Or how would you treat them?

Professional: I mean obviously if I'm with you I'm not tripping.

If I'm not with you and your trying to get with me, it depends on if you and your child's father are having issues. It depends on if I see something in you that makes me feel I want you. Then it's the behavior of the kids. Were they raised properly and in good respectful taste?

How would I treat them? It depends on how I say how they were raised. But I would do what I can to be a good remodel. I just feel like women should not force no one to play daddy or to take on all the responsibilities of someone else's. A lot of women say they want a man that's going to take care of her and her kids. Those are the child's father duties not mine. Let me wanna do it. Don't just plug in to do so. Don't obligate me to do it. But I most likely will be what I need to be when it all comes down.

Thug: I don't know. I mean I'm not tripping, but don't try to give me the role of daddy. I hope they are not clock blockers and bad as hell. Shit, I probably got a kid myself so I mean we just gotta do what we gotta do. As long as you're not still in love or sexing with your BD; it's all good. I can't deal with no more than two though.

If you get a message from your ex saying she loves you, how would you respond or would you?

Professional: I mean it depends on if I'm with someone or not and how me and her relationship was before. If I got a woman, I would definitely ask her to respect my girl. But if I wasn't in a relationship and we were on good terms, I probably still love her no matter what anyway. I would tell her I love her back and ask if she was ok. And tell her thank you. Never know what a person is going through. Anything could be on her mind that needs attention other than sex and physical things. Could save her life, never know.

Thug: I don't know it depends on what type of relationship we got. If I love her I tell her I love her back it ain't got a really mean too much of nothing. But if I don't love her I ain't going to say nothing back. No need for me to respond or anything if I don't love her back if I don't feel the same way. But there could be the ones that you just love no matter what and wouldn't let anything happen to him. But I definitely would not disrespect wifey or whoever I'm with not going any further.

Do our feelings and emotions count? Like do they mean anything to you? Do they affect any decisions you make? Do you think about them before you make certain decisions?

Professional: The reason why I say a woman's feelings and emotions matter is because when it comes to a woman there born to be emotional creatures. Mother, grandmothers, girlfriends, wives, and even daughters show us everything we need to know about emotions and feelings. You just have to pay attention. If you look at how a man teaches a boy, when he is younger, what's the first thing he tells his son, "Boys don't cry." We are taught to be lions, have heart, take care of your family, and show no signs of weakness. Never show your emotions and fight. As a woman, when she teaches her daughter, she teaches her how to love care and to just have a great heart. I hope this can help you. That's why I say your definitely supposed to respect a woman's feelings and emotions.

Thug: I mean, a woman's feelings do matter. I'm not going to say it don't. But it's funny y'all want men to care about your feelings. But when it comes to ours with certain things it's ignored and it don't matter. Just like with you making one sided decisions like having a child and you ignore our feelings against it. I think men start to process that your feelings don't count. If we are in a relationship together, then yes, it definitely matters but only if it's both ways.

If you could change one thing about women or a woman you may dating, what would it be and why?

Professional: Assumptions, because y'all get so lost into your assumption that you trick yourself. The devil attacks that and makes you say and do crazy shit. And you ruin everything we built.

Sometimes, it may be nothing wrong until you start to do so. It could be from your past, but it becomes a plague and infects all your relationships. You be so deep in that you place the fault on the man and here's the sickness.

Thug: That's a good one. I would say a woman's attitude. I feel y'all can be bipolar at times. Y'all are so mixy that it's hard to tell who you are every day. A man never knows what he'll get until it's too late. We don't like the mixy attitudes. It's a turn off and it makes us wanna stay out all night, come in when you sleep or worse sleep out because we don't feel like the drama. It's like you're always in your feelings or mad about some shit for no reason.

If it's one thing you can change about yourself in a relationship, what would it be and why?

Professional: Understanding, I mean I got understanding it's just I feel maybe there can be more of it. I feel women make it hard for us to try to understand sometimes. Y'all ask us to try to understand and when we do it's like we are a bother or like we will never understand. That's why I tell y'all to keep it to yourselves. So, tell me how are we supposed to then, if you don't allow us too? I guess that's what we supposed to understand; that we'll never understand. Maybe you just want to see the effort more or that'll make the relationship better on my part.

Thug: My urge of temptation. I think if I just communicate more maybe you'll spice things up. I just need to think of things to do if I get bored or to use to the sex. I think men would rather see you make the effort to change things up but maybe I can try harder to help you. Maybe this will help kill the urge of wanting something new or wanting to prove myself to something. Or even when things get bad I can kill that temptation and weather the storm.

Would you hit a woman back if she hits you?

Professional: I feel no woman should put their hands on a man. Especially if you don't want to get hit back. My objective is to defuse the situation before any of that transpire. I probably would let the first one or two times go. Depending on where you hit me. I've seen women hit dudes in their face with punches, not slaps, even though I've seen the slaps a well. It depends on if you're hitting me with your fists or with an object. Then you might get beat up cause that means you're crazy as hell and you obviously weighed out the outcome.

Thug: Don't hit me or I'ma probably hit yo ass back. I don't have time for the bull shit, fa real. If I don't hit you; don't hit me. That's my rule point blank. If you raise your hands to me, it means you probably done this before. Which means you know there's a chance I will hit ya back.

Summary

There's so much that can be covered but can't give you all of it. I gotta give you some homework to do on your own ladies. Just as much as you want to understand us, we want to understand y'all as well. You have to become open minded and dig deep into the reasons why we are the way we are. But also be understanding as well, because I know you were brought up feeling we are supposed to put in all the work. Like we are supposed to make it right no matter what the situation is. Whether we are unhappy or not we are supposed to just deal with the situation. Maybe back in the day that was what was happening, but not today.

I think it has come to a time where we men, just get tired of the abuse women dish out. There's no songs saying when a man's fed up. Only songs saying when a woman's fed up or tired. Cause everyone puts a woman's feelings and emotions before everything. Ladies you got to realize ours are just as important as yours. It's not just about you. If you take this book and apply it to your life, you'll see a major change in your relationship. You'll also see the part you played in the ups and downs in your past relationships and in your current on as well.

It'll be shocking once you discover how easily things could've been different. Also, I hope you didn't just read this book and put it down. You gotta really dissect each chapter and meditate on it. Just like the Bible. Sometimes you gotta study what's being read. I encourage you to read this book a few times. You can even read a chapter a day or a week after. Let these jewels become natural works. The more you read and study the better it'll stick. Like I said. Don't be afraid of change, accept it and conquer the challenge. What else do you have to lose?

By trying what is written, trust the process and have faith in it. Don't let no one tell you no different. People who know it all will try to persuade you differently. Try it for yourself and make your own analysis. I believe it's a guarantee and you'll recommend it to someone else. Studying and taking the time to understand a man, just as we gotta do you, would make life so much easier. The other easiest way to handle it is to run away and give up.

I, myself, have fought for relationships to work, but realized it was always one sided. It's like you beautifully made women of the Earth feel you shouldn't have to put the work in. I wrote this book to help you help us to become better, but also to help you keep the man you desire to be and stay with. I have a daughter and a niece and I want them to understand who they are dealing with. I want them to be able to maneuver and not be lost when it comes to a man. This is not by far a book that's meant for you to bow to a man, but to stand up and over stand him. Don't get caught up on how others feel it should be; manly women. You can look at them and analyze their advice just by their situation. Are they in a relationship? Are they happy? Questions you can ask yourself and so on.

BE DIFFERENT... UNDER/OVER STANDING... OPEN MINDED... BE PATIENT... STUDY... MAKE THE CORRECT CHOICES AND DECISIONS... LOVE YOURSELF... PUT GOD FIRST... HAVE

FAITH AND BELIEVE... BUT VALUE AND TAKE NOTHING LESS THAN WHAT GOD GIVES YOU... BUT, ALSO BE A FIGHTER...

Author's Note

I HOPE THAT EVERYONE CAN TRULY TAKE IN THE TRUTHS
THAT ARE IN THIS BOOK. YES I EXPECT PEOPLE NOT TO
AGREE WITH EVERYTHING THE EYES SEE AND THE MIND
TAKE IN. BUT BE VERY OPEN-MINDED GET OUT OF THAT
BOX WE WERE TAUGHT TO STAY IN. DON'T BE AFRAID TO
TRY NEW THINGS EVEN IF YOU DON'T BELIEVE. YOUR NOT
GOING TO BE ABLE TO BE A BELIEVER IF YOU DON'T TRY IT
OUT. YOU MAY SURPRISE YOURSELF TO ONLY DISCOVER
THAT THE THINGS YOU THOUGHT YOU DIDN'T AGREE
WITH, OR DID NOT BELIEVE WAS REALLY REAL. YOU MAY
DISCOVER A WHOLE NEW BEGINNING AND A NEW START
OF HAPPINESS IT ONLY TAKES A LITTLE FAITH. OVERCOME
YOUR FEAR OF FAILURE AND JUST ASK YOURSELF "WHAT
IS THE WORST THAT CAN HAPPEN?".

WE CAN'T KNOCK NOTHING UNTIL WE TRY IT!!!!!!

NOTES

Biographies

bornrich.com. (2020). "Pablo Escobar Net Worth. Retrieved from

http://www.bornrich.com/pablo-escobar.html#:~:text=Pablo%20E
scobar%20net%20worth%20is%20estimated%20at%20%2430,
the%20main%20source%20of%20Pablo%20Escobar%20ne
t%20worth.

celebritynetworth.com. (2020). Griselda Blanco. Retrieved from
https://www.celebritynetworth.com/richest-businessmen/richest-
criminals/griselda-blanco-net-worth/

celebritynetworth.com. (2020) Freeway Rick Ross Net Worth.
https://www.celebritynetworth.com/richest-businessmen/richest-
criminals/freeway-rick-ross-net-worth/

businessinsider.com (2020) The US got 'El Chapo' Guzman — now it has to get his
$14 billion. Retrieved from https://www.businessinsider.com/el-chapo-
guzman-4-billion-the-us-got-now-it-has-to-get-his-12019-2

murderpedia.org. (2020). Edward Theodore Gein. Retrieved from
http://www.murderpedia.org/male.G/g/gein-edward.htm

murderpedia.org. (2020) Dennis Lynn Rader. Retrieve from
http://www.murderpedia.org/male.R/r/rader-dennis.htm

murderpedia.org. (2020) Charles Myles Manson. Retrieved from

    http://www.murderpedia.org/male.M/m/manson-charles.htm

murderpedia.org. (2002) Nannie Doss. Retrieved from

    http://www.murderpedia.org/female.D/d/doss-nannie.htm

murderpedia.org. (2020) Albert Hamilton Fish. Retrieve from

    http://www.murderpedia.org/male.F/f/fish-albert.htm

murderpedia.org. (2020) Katherine Mary Knight. Retrieved from

    http://www.murderpedia.org/female.K/k/knight-katherine.htm

webmd.com. (2020) Condoms. Retrieved from https://www.webmd.com/sex/

    birth-control/birth-controlcondoms#:~:text=When%20used%20properly

    %2C%20male%20condoms%20are%20about%2098%25,condoms%20are

    %20about%2095%25%20effective%20when%20used%20properly.

plannedparenthood.org, (2020) How effective are condoms? Retrieved from

    https://www.plannedparenthood.org/learn/birth-control/condom/how-

    effective-are-condoms

Celebrities

atlantablackstar.com. (2020) Keyshia Ka'Oir's Bond With Gucci Mane Seen as

    Unbreakable by Fans. Retrieved from https://atlantablackstar.com/

    2019/01/24/keyshia-kaoirs-bond-with-gucci-mane-seen-as-unbreakable-

    by-fans/

Definitions

1. medlineplus.com. Kegel exercises - self-care. Retrieved from
    https://medlineplus.gov/ency/patientinstructions/000141.htm

2. lexico.com. (2020) "friend" Retrieved from https://
    www.lexico.com/en/definition/friend

3. lexion.com. (2020) "associate" Retrieved from
    https://www.lexico.com/en/definition/associate

4. Merriam-Webster.com. (2020) "communication" Retrieved from
    https://www.merriam-webster.com/dictionary/
    communication

5. lexion.com. (2020) "nagging" Retrieved from
    https://www.lexico.com/en/definition/nagging

6. lexion.com. (2020) "nag" Retrieved from https://www.lexico.com/
    en/definition/nag

7. lexion.com. (2020) "petty" Retrieved from https://
    www.lexico.com/en/definition/petty

8. lexico.com. (2020) "assumption" Retrieved from
    https://www.lexico.com/en/definition/assumption

9. lexico.com. (2020) "self-respect" Retrieved from
    https://www.lexico.com/en/definition/self-respect

10. lexico.com. (2020) "change" Retrieved from https://
    www.lexico.com/en/definition/change

11. lexico.com. (2020) "habit" Retrieved from https://
    www.lexico.com/en/definition/habit

12. lexico.com. (2020) "flaw" Retrieved from https://www.lexico.com/
    en/definition/flaw

13. lexico.com. (2020) "sacrifice" Retrieved from
    https://www.lexico.com/en/definition/sacrifice

14. lexico.com. (2020) "protector" Retrieved from
    https://www.lexico.com/en/definition/protector

15. lexico.com. (2020) "thug" Retrieved from https://www.lexico.com/
    en/definition/thug

16. lexico.com. (2020) "hustler" Retrieved from https://
    www.lexico.com/en/definition/hustler

17. lexico.com. (2020) "jealous" Retrieved from https://
    www.lexico.com/en/definition/jealous

18. lexico.com. (2020) "jealousy" Retrieved from
    https://www.lexico.com/en/definition/jealousy

19. lexico.com. (2020) "fear" Retrieved from https://www.lexico.com/
    en/definition/fear

20. lexico.com. (2020) "police" Retrieved from https://
    www.lexico.com/en/definition/police

21. lexico.com. (2020) "hate" Retrieved from https://www.lexico.com/
    en/definition/hate

22. kingjamesbibleonline.com. (2020) Retrieved from
    https://www.kingjamesbibleonline.org/search.php?
    q=to+hate+someone+is+the+same+as+murder&hs=1

23. salary.com. (2020) Police Patrol Officer Salary in the United
    States. Retrieved from https://www.salary.com/research/
    salary/benchmark/police-patrol-officer-salary

24. lexico.com. (2020) "pressure" Retrieved from
    https://www.lexico.com/en/definition/pressure

25. lexico.com (2020) "feelings" Retrieved from
    https://www.lexico.com/en/definition/feeling

26. lexico.com. (2020) "emotions" Retrieved from
    https://www.lexico.com/en/definition/emotion

27. lexico.com. (2020) "limbic system" Retrieved from
    https://www.lexico.com/en/definition/limbic_system

28. Merriam-Webster.com. (2020) "alexithymic" Retrieved from
    https://www.merriam-webster.com/medical/alexithymia#:~
    :text=Medical%20Definition%20of%20alexithymia.%20%3A%2
    0inability%20to%20identify,they%20have%20difficulty%20di
    fferentiating%20emotions%20and%20verbalizing%20them.

29. alexithymia.us. (2020) "alexithymia" Retrieved from
    https://www.alexithymia.us/dictionary/Alexithymia

30. lexico.com. (2020) "sociopath" Retrieved from
    https://www.lexico.com/en/definition/sociopath

31. lexico.com. (2020) "psychopath" Retrieved from
    https://www.lexico.com/en/definition/psychopath

32. lexico.com. (2020) "alter ego" Retrieved from
    https://www.lexico.com/en/definition/alter_ego

33. healthyplace.com. (2020) Most Famous Sociopaths To Ever Walk
    The Earth. Retrieved From https://www.healthyplace.com/personality-
    disorders/sociopath/most-famous-sociopaths-to-ever-walk-the-earth

Medical Terminology

ncbi.nlm.nih.gov. (2020) "Alexithymia and Its Associations With Depression,
    Suicidality, and Aggression: An Overview of the Literature" Retrieved
    from https://www.ncbi.nlm.nih.gov/pmc/articles/PMC6470633/

Movies

Kirkman, Robert. The Walking Dead. Orange, CA :Image Comics, 2010

        Future & Silver, J. (Producers). Director X. (2018) Superfly. Sony

        Pictures. Andrew Kosove, Broderick Johnson. Mark Burg. Love Don't

        Cost A Thing. Warner Bros., 2003

Scott, D. (Producer). Hughes, A. & Hughes, A. (Directors). (1993). Menace to

        Society. Los Angeles, California, USA. New Line Cinema

Slater, T., & Walt Disney Productions. (1991). Disney's Beauty And The

        Beast.Racine, Wis.: Western Pub. Company.

Finerman, W., Starkey, S., & Tisch, S. (Producers). Zemeckis, R. Zemeckis

        (Director). (1994). Forrest Gump. Paramount Pictures.

Alonso, V., D'Esposito, L., Feige, K., Fine, A., Grant, D., Kyle, C., Lee, S., Maisel,

        D., & Whitcher, P. (Producers). Branagh, K. (Director). (2011). Thor: The

        Gauardian. Marvel Studios.

Music

Young Buck. Shorty Want to Ride. Straight Outta Cashville. G-Unit Records. August
24, 2004. 50 Cents. She Money XL. Denaun Porter, Lil Jon. Red Spyda.

The Beatles. Helter Skelter. The Beatles. Apple Records. 1968. Martin, G.

Shys Debiocci. "Suppose Ta Be Us". Tunecore, 2019

Nas. "Oochie Wally". The Essential Nas. Ez Elpee. Ill Will Records & Columbia

Records.2013

www.ingramcontent.com/pod-product-compliance
Lightning Source LLC
Chambersburg PA
CBHW060004100426
42740CB00010B/1387